PENNSYLVANIA RULES OF EVIDENCE HANDBOOK

with Common
Objections & Evidentiary Foundations

2024

(Rules last amended Nov. 2023)

Professor John Barkai

Colors on the cover match the colors of the state flag

Regarding copyright – there is none. In addition, I give you permission to freely copy and use other sections of this handbook, including the sections on objections and evidentiary foundations, under a Creative Commons Attribution (CCBY) 4.0 License, which essentially means that you may use, share, or adapt the information in these pages for any purpose, even commercial, if you give "appropriate credit" and indicate changes you made, if any. Please cite the material as: John Barkai, Pennsylvania Rules of Evidence Handbook with Common Objections & Evidentiary Foundations.

Where are the cartons that were in previous editions of this handbook? Those evidence, negotiation, and ADR cartoons were included before I published two separate cartoon books. Now those cartoons, and many more, are in the cartoon books which are also sold on Amazon. If you are dying to seeing the cartoons, email me and I will send you an e-copy.

Formatting. There seems to be no standard formatting style for presenting the rules of evidence. This handbook uses formatting intended to make the understanding and application of the rules as clear as possible - but clarity and ease of understanding of the rules of evidence by using the text alone is almost impossible..

Disclaimer: The author and publisher are offering no legal advice. Your trial judge may view the law and foundations differently. The law is whatever the judge in your case says it is. Any errors in this book are mine.

Corrections, omissions, suggestions?
See any or have some? Contact me at barkai@hawaii.edu

Common Citation Forms: Pa. R. E. xxx.

Amendments and additions (effective) to rules:
2023 – R101, 102, 103(amended only the comments), 201(only comments)
2022 – R404(b) & 803(3)
2021 – R413
2020 - R901(11)

For Amendments to the Pennsylvania Rules of Evidence see, https://www.pacourts.us/courts/supreme-court/committees/rules-committees/committee-on-rules-of-evidence

Pennsylvania Rules of Evidence Handbook with Common Objections & Evidentiary Foundations

Professor John Barkai
William S. Richardson School of Law
University of Hawaii
Honolulu, HI 96822
Dec. 2023

ISBN: 9798681863427

INTRODUCTION

This handbook of the Pennsylvania Rules of Evidence Handbook was designed to be brought to court and be at your side in the office.

Besides the rules of evidence, the **"added value"** in this handbook is the following sections:

A) **Making and Responding to Common Objections** (16 pages)
- a discussion of the most common objections
- a list of the most common objections

B) **Evidentiary Foundations and Impeachment** (over 60 pages)
- 25 examples of the most common evidentiary foundations
- a brief discussion of differing standards for authenticating digital evidence (such as email, text messages, social media sites, internet sites).

The sample foundation and impeachment questions are "bare-bones" foundations which include the minimum questions and answers necessary to get testimony or exhibits admitted into evidence

Professor John Barkai

SUMMARY OF CONTENTS

Introduction iii
Summary of Contents..iv
Expanded Table of Contents v
Sample Pages from Deeper in the Handbook viii
Pennsylvania Rules of Evidence (by number and title) xiii
Most Commonly Used Hearsay Sub-Sections xv
Pennsylvania Rules of Evidence (full rules) 1-34

Appendix

Making and Responding to Common Objections A-1
   A List of Common Objections A-15
Evidentiary Foundations A-17
   Evidentiary Foundations Index A-18
   Sample Foundational Questions (Predicates) A-35
   Digital Evidence – Electronically Stored Information – ESI.A-62
History and Restyling of The Federal Rules of Evidence.....................A-78
Teaching Evidence since 4 B.C. A-79
Other Evidence Books in This Series by John Barkai A-80
Dedication A-82
About the Author A-82

Expanded Table of Contents for Appendix

Making and Responding to Common Objections A-1
Why Do Lawyers Object? A-1
Make an Objection in Four Steps A-2
How to Respond to an Objection A-2
If You are a Judge Who Has to Rule on the Objection A-3
Multiple Lawyers and Multiple Clients A-3
Judges Apply the Rules of Evidence More Loosely in Nonjury Trials. ... A-3
The Key to Objection is Rule 103 .... A-3
Important Points about Rule 103 .... A-4
Rule 103. Rulings on Evidence A-4
Objections - Rules - Constitutional Issues A-5
Motions in Limine A-5
Phrases that Suggest Inadmissible Information A-6
Inadequate Objections A-6
Offers of Proof A-6
Nonjury Trials – Seldom Reversed A-7
Common Phrases from Court Opinions A-7
Common Objections to the Form of the Question A-8
    Argumentative (Harassing, Badgering) A-8
    Asked and Answered A-8
    Assuming Facts Not in Evidence A-9
    Beyond the Scope A-9
    Compound Question A-10
    Cumulative A-10
    Lack of Foundation A-10
    Leading Question A-11
    Motion to strike A-11
    Narrative Question A-12
    Non-Responsive Answer A-12
    Speculation A-13
    Vague and Ambiguous Question A-13
Golden Rule A-13
Speaking Objections A-14
Coaching the Witness A-14
Relevance A-14
A Few Useful Definitions A-15
    Stipulation A-15
    Offer of Proof A-15
    Motion in Limine A-15
    Limited Admissibility A-15
    Intrinsic Impeachment A-15
    Extrinsic A-15
    Collateral A-15
A List of Common Objections A-16

Evidentiary Foundations A-17
Foundations – Laying the Foundation - Predicates A-17
Evidentiary Foundations Index..A-18
Bare-Bones Foundations A-20
Admissibility v. Weight A-21
Example of Admissibility and Weight A-21
3 Simple Questions A-22
Steps for Introducing Exhibits...A-23
The Common Evidentiary Foundations..A-25
The Phrases to Move Evidence into a Trial.......................................A-26
Useful Points to Remember..A-27
    Into Evidence A-27
    Make an Offer of Proof..A-27
    Hearsay Within Hearsay A-27
    Public Records Do Not Have to Be Open to The Public A-27
    Compute Generated Record Is Not Hearsay..............................A-27
    Emails Offered to Show Notice, Knowledge or Fear Are Not Hearsay ..A-27
    Demonstrative Evidence A-27
    Chain of Custody A-27
    Distinctive Characteristics A-27
    Authenticate with Personal Knowledge and Distinctive Characteristics.A-28
    Affidavits Are Hearsay and Inadmissible at Trial A-28
    Harrowing A-28
    OTP – Offered to Prove A-28
    Rules Do Not Explain How to Introduce Evidence in Court........A-28
    Laying A Foundation Is Like A Sport A-28
    Mark, Show, Approach, Foundational Questions, Offer A-28
    Magic Words..A-29
    Speak in Generic Terms...A-29
    Publish Means to Show Them Now...A-29
    Chain of Custody Is Only for Fungible Items or Samples to Test A-29
    Basic Tasks A Trial Lawyer Should Be Able to Do A-29
    Best Evidentiary Foundation Resources A-29
    Important Evidence Rules to Guide You - 103, 104, 901, 612,
        613, 801, 803(6), 901, 902(11), 902(13&14), 105, 106, 1006 A-30
    Opponent Has the Burden on The Issue of Trustworthiness A-31
Foundation & Impeachment Examples A-32
    Nita Liquor Commission Facts A-33
    Officer Bier's Report A-34
    Diagram of Cut-Rate Liquor Store Area......................................A-35
    Photograph of A Scene A-36
    Diagram of The Scene A-37
    Real Evidence – Thunderbird Wine Bottle A-38
    Offering A Contract into Evidence A-39
    Refreshing Memory – Anything A-40

Writing Used to Refresh Memory – R612	A-42
Refreshing Memory with A Leading Question	A-43
Recorded Recollection (Author's Rule)	A-44
Business Records - Custodian of Records – R803(6)	A-46
Business Records Are KRAP	A-47
Self-Authenticating Business Records Form - Texas	A-48
Demonstrative Evidence - Similar to The Real Item	A-49
Impeachment - Prior Written Inconsistent Statement	A-50
Impeachment by Omission	A-52
Impeachment by Inconsistent Oral Deposition	A-54
Impeachment - Inconsistent Oral Deposition - Short Form	A-55
Impeachment - Inconsistent Oral Deposition - Long Form	A-56
Impeachment - Inconsistent Oral Statement	A-57
Learned Treatises Use on Direct Exam – FRE 803(18)	A-58
3 Key Points for Using Learned Treatises	A-59
Learned Treatises: Use on Cross -	A-60
Voicemail and Phone Conversations	A-61
Digital Evidence – Electronically Stored Information – ESI	A-63
A Variety of Different Standards	A-63
Distinctive Characteristics and Circumstantial Evidence	A-65
Presenting Digital Evidence from A Cell Phone in Court	A-66
Digital Evidence and Self-Authentication	A-67
Digital Evidence Foundations	A-63
Email – Outgoing	A-68
Email – Incoming	A-69
Text Message – Received by Witness	A-70
Social Media: Facebook, Instagram, Snapchat, Twitter	A-71
Internet Website – Web Posting	A-72
Fax – Incoming	A-73
Foundation for Expert Opinion	A-74
History and Restyling of The Federal Rules of Evidence	A-78
Teaching Evidence since 4 B.C.	A-79
Other Evidence Books in This Series by John Barkai	A-80
Dedication	A-82
About the Author	A-82

SAMPLE PAGE FROM DEEPER IN THE HANDBOOK

Make an Objection in Four Steps
1) Stand up.
2) Say, "Objection ____ " (Fill in the blank with your reason).
3) Identify your specific objection.
    a) At a minimum, say the topic type
        (Hearsay, Relevance, Improper Impeachment, Improper Character, Lack of Foundation, Leading Question, etc.)
    b) State the evidence rule number if you know it (404, 608, etc.).
    c) A combination of the above
        ("Objection, Improper Impeachment, R613")
4) Stop talking and listen to the judge.
    Be prepared to state reasons for your objection and to make an argument to support your position.

How to Respond to An Objection?
1) Speak to the judge, not the lawyer who objected.
2) Explain to the judge why your evidence should be admissible. ("Your Honor, that statement is not hearsay because I am not offering it for the truth but rather to show notice.")
3) If you recognize that you did not lay an appropriate foundation for the evidence explain that you will do that. ("Your Honor, I will lay the foundation.")
4) If you recognize that the opposing counsel was objecting to the form of your question, which most often happens on your direct examination, simply say, "I'll rephrase." Rephrase the question and move on with your witness examination. Do not get sidetracked by the opposing counsel who might have objected just to throw you off track.
5) For any physical piece of evidence, statement, or testimony that you will be introducing, prepare in advance and have a reason why you believe that evidence is admissible. Be ready to make that argument to the judge.
6) If the objection is to relevance, and you think you will be able to show that it is relevant, say to the judge "I will connect it up in a few questions Your Honor." Such a statement is equivalent of saying "trust me." If you do that, you'd better connect it up or the judge will not trust you in the future.

SAMPLE PAGE FROM DEEPER IN THE HANDBOOK

A List of Common Possible Objections

Ambiguous	Improper opinion
Argumentative	Improper rehabilitation
Asked and answered	Inadmissible opinion
Assumes facts not in evidence	Incompetent witness
Authentication	Incomplete Inflammatory
Badgering	Insufficient foundation
Best evidence	Irrelevant (Relevance)
Beyond the scope	Lack of foundation
Bias	Lack of personal knowledge
Bolstering	Leading question
Calls for a conclusion	Misleading
Calls for speculation	Misquotes a witness or exhibit
Chain of custody	Misquotes evidence
Collateral	Misstates witness
Competence	More prejudicial than probative
Compound question	Motion to strike
Compromise / Settlement offer	Narrative
Confrontation (lack of)	(Question calls for a narrative)
Confusing	Narrative answer
Counsel is testifying	Non-responsive
Cumulative	Nothing pending
Document speaks for itself	Outside the scope of cross
Expert (Improper opinion)	Overly broad or general
Expert (not qualified)	Parole evidence rule
Habit	Personal knowledge
Harassing the witness	Prejudice (unfair)
Hearsay	Privilege communication
Hypothetical question misused	Relevance
Improper character evidence	Speculation/ Opinion/ Lack of
Improper characterization	personal knowledge
Improper impeachment	Unintelligible
	Vague

There are many more possible objections,
limited only by the lawyer's imagination.

Judges and the local legal culture in your jurisdiction may have other rules or approaches to objections that are not touched on in this handbook. Ask around and learn about them.

SAMPLE PAGE FROM DEEPER IN THE HANDBOOK

Steps for Introducing Exhibits

> **Preliminary steps are:**
> 1) Have the exhibit marked for identification
> 2) Show the proposed exhibit to opposing counsel
> 3) Ask permission to approach the witness with the proposed exhibit

1. History - How the witness knows the exhibit.
Offer some testimony that the witness <u>knows</u> or is <u>familiar with</u> the evidence – such as a document, physical item, photo, diagram, scene, text message, email - or recalls the statement. Even if the witness has only seen the exhibit once before or has just been to the scene shown in the photograph once before, <u>once is enough</u>.

2. The Litany (a ritualistic repetition of foundational questions)
a) Ask the court clerk to **mark the item** (using numbers or letters). The clerk will decide which system to use. In more serious cases in the jurisdiction's higher courts (typically where jury trials are allowed), exhibits are usually required to be marked at least before trial starts, and often during pretrial conferences.
b) **Show opposing counsel** (this will prevent interruptions) and say, "Let the record reflect that I am showing the defense what has been marked as plaintiff's proposed exhibit number one."
c) Ask the judge for **permission to approach** the witness. "May I approach the witness?"
- Q: "**I show you what has been marked as** Plaintiff's (Prosecution's) (Defense's) proposed exhibit # x (or exhibit #x for identification purposes) **and ask whether you can identify it**" (You expect a "yes" answer here.)
- Q: "**What is it?**" (They describe it in general terms. "It is the contract/photo of the scene/weapon recovered/drugs seized/diagram of the area/etc.")
- Q: "**How do you know that?**" (They answer – "I recognize it. It has my signature on it. / I have been there many times before. / I put my initials on it and the defendant's name/etc.")

SAMPLE PAGE FROM DEEPER IN THE HANDBOOK

3. Show Condition or Comparison or Accuracy

Some comparison must be made between the exhibit in court and when the witness became familiar with the exhibit out-of-court. Of the examples that follow, only one such question is necessary.

- "Is this in the **same** condition as when you... [first saw it...seized it...etc.]?"
- "Is this in the **same or substantially** the same condition.... as when you…" (for item or document)
- "Is it a **fair and accurate representation of** the ... **as it was that day**?" (for diagram or pictures)
- "**Has it changed** in any significant way?"
- "**How does it compare** to the item you saw that day?"

4. Move or Offer the Exhibit into Evidence

"Your honor, **I offer the exhibit into evidence**." - or, "I move the exhibit into evidence."

You could instead say, "I offer proposed exhibit # 1 into evidence as exhibit # 1," but why make it so confusing? Just say, "I offer the exhibit into evidence."

The judge <u>might</u> ask the opposing counsel, "Any objections?" but the opponent should object immediately after the proponent offers the exhibit if there is an objection to the admissibility (not the weight). The judge should allow "voir dire" (immediate cross examination limited to the foundation and the admissibility) by the opponent of the exhibit.

SAMPLE PAGE FROM DEEPER IN THE HANDBOOK

Authentication of Text Message – An Example

Text Message

Received by Witness

Do you know Y?

Do you communicate with Y on a regular basis?

In what ways to you communicate with Y?

Did you receive a text message from the Y [recently; on or about _ date, on the topic of ..., etc.]?

Would you recognize a printout of the message if you were to see it again?

Let me show you what has been marked as proposed exhibit # 1. Do you recognize it?

What is it? [Ans: A screenshot from my cell phone]

How do you know that this is a message from Y? [It is similar to other messages I have received from Y in that ...]

How did it appear when it arrived on your phone? [Showed up under the name and with the picture I had previously assigned to Y]

What other distinctive characteristics did you notice about the message? [provide as many as distinctive characteristics possible]

Is it a fair and accurate representation of the text message you received [recently; on or about _ date, on the topic of visiting your son, etc.]?

Has it been altered in any way?

I would like to enter the proposed exhibit into evidence

PENNSYLVANIA RULES OF EVIDENCE

(Rules last amended in Nov. 2023)

ARTICLE I. GENERAL PROVISIONS
Rule 101 Scope, Adoption and Citation, and Construction of Rules. 1
Rule 102 Application of Rules..1
Rule 103 Rulings of Evidence...1
Rule 104 Preliminary Questions 2
Rule 105 Limited Admissibility Evidence That Is Not Admissible Against Other
   Parties or for Other Purposes..2
Rule 106 Remainder of or Related Writings or Recorded Statements 2
Rule 107 Rule of Optional Completeness..2

ARTICLE II. JUDICIAL NOTICE
Rule 201 Judicial Notice of Adjudicative Facts 3

ARTICLE III. PRESUMPTIONS
Rule 301 Presumptions 3

ARTICLE IV. RELEVANCY AND ITS LIMITS.
Rule 401 Test for Relevant Evidence 4
Rule 402 Generally Admissibility of Relevant Evidence 4
Rule 403 Excluding Relevant Evidence for Prejudice, Confusion, or Other Reasons 4
Rule 404 Character Evidence; Other Crimes, Wrongs, or Acts....................................5
Rule 405 Methods of Proving Character..6
Rule 406 Habit; Routine Practice...6
Rule 407 Subsequent Remedial Measures 7
Rule 408 Compromise Offers and Negotiations 7
Rule 409 Offers to Pay Medical and Similar Expenses 7
Rule 410 Pleas, Plea Discussions, and Related Statements 8
Rule 411 Liability Insurance..8
Rule 412 Sex Offense Cases: The Victim's Sexual Behavior or Predisposition [Not
   Adopted – but PA uses 18 Pa.C.S 1304] 9
Rule 413 Evidence of Immigration Status...9

ARTICLE V. PRIVILEGES.
Rule 501 Privileges..10
Rule 502 Attorney-Client Privilege and Work Product; Limitations on Waiver
   [Not Adopted] 10

ARTICLE VI. WITNESSES.
Rule 601 Competency 11
Rule 602 Need for Personal Knowledge..11
Rule 603 Oath or Affirmation to Testify Truthfully 11
Rule 604 Interpreters 11
Rule 605 Judge's Competency as a Witness 11
Rule 606 Juror's Competency as a Witness...12
Rule 607 Who May Impeach a Witness, Evidence to Impeach a Witness 12
Rule 608 A Witness's Character for Truthfulness or Untruthfulness 13
Rule 609 Impeachment by Evidence of a Criminal Conviction 14
Rule 610 Religious Beliefs or Opinions 14
Rule 611 Mode and Order of Examining Witnesses and Presenting Evidence.............15
Rule 612 Writing or Other Item Used to Refresh a Witness's Memory...................16
Rule 613 Witness's Prior Inconsistent Statement to Impeach; Witness's
  Prior Consistent Statement to Rehabilitate 17
Rule 614 Court's Calling or Examining a Witness 18
Rule 615 Sequestering Witnesses...18

ARTICLE VII. OPINIONS AND EXPERT TESTIMONY
Rule 701 Opinion Testimony by Lay Witnesses 19
Rule 702 Testimony by Expert Witnesses 19
Rule 703 Bases of an Expert's Opinion Testimony 19
Rule 704 Opinion on an Ultimate Issue 19
Rule 705 Disclosing the Facts or Data Underlying an Expert's Opinion 19
Rule 706 Court-Appointed Expert Witnesses 19

ARTICLE VIII. HEARSAY.
Rule 801 Hearsay..20
Rule 802 The Rule Against Hearsay 20
Rule 803 Exceptions to the Rule Against Hearsay—Regardless of Whether the
  Declarant Is Available as a Witness 20
Rule 803.1 Exceptions to the Rule Against Hearsay—Testimony of Declarant
  Necessary 25
Rule 804 Exceptions to the Rule Against Hearsay—When the Declarant Is
  Unavailable as a Witness 26
Rule 805 Hearsay Within Hearsay...28
Rule 806 Attacking and Supporting the Declarant's Credibility 28
Rule 807 Residual Exception [Not Adopted]..28

ARTICLE IX. AUTHENTICATION AND IDENTIFICATION.
Rule 901 Authenticating or Identifying Evidence 28
Rule 902 Evidence That Is Self-Authenticating 30
Rule 903 Subscribing Witness's Testimony 32

ARTICLE IX. CONTENTS OF WRITINGS, RECORDINGS, AND PHOTOGRAPHS.
Rule 1001 Definitions That Apply to This Article 33
Rule 1002 Requirements of the Original...33
Rule 1003 Admissibility of Duplicates 33
Rule 1004 Admissibility of Other Evidence of Content 33
Rule 1005 Copies of Public Records to Prove Content...34
Rule 1006 Summaries to Prove Content 34
Rule 1007 Testimony or Statement of a Party to Prove Content............................34
Rule 1008 Functions of the Court and Jury 34

THE MOST COMMONLY USED PENNSYLVANIA HEARSAY SUB-SECTIONS

Rule 801. Hearsay 20

Rule 802. The Rule Against Hearsay 20

Rule 803. Hearsay Exceptions – (Availability Immaterial) 20
   (1) Present Sense Impression 20
   (2) Excited Utterance 20
   (3) Then-Existing Mental, Emotional, or Physical Condition ...21
   (4) Statements Made for Medical Diagnosis or Treatment 21
   (6) Records of A Regularly Conducted Activity (business records)..21
   (8) Public Records 22
   (17) Market Reports and Similar Commercial Publications 23
   (25) An Opposing Party's Statement (Admissions)...................24

Rule 803.1 Hearsay Exceptions – (Declarant Testifies) 25
   (1) Prior Inconsistent Statement (under oath – or otherwise) ...25
   (2) Prior Statement of Identification by Declarant-Witness 25
   (3) Recorded Recollection of Declarant-Witness.......................25
   (4) Prior Statement – (declarant claims inability to remember).26

Rule 804(b). Exceptions 26
   (1) Former testimony 27
   (2) Statement Under the Belief of Imminent death (dying declaration)..27
   (3) Statement Against Interest 27

Rule 805. Hearsay Within Hearsay 28

PENNSYLVANIA RULES OF EVIDENCE
(Amended in 2023; restyled in 2014)

ARTICLE I. GENERAL PROVISIONS

Rule 101. Scope, Adoption and Citation, and Construction of Rules.
(a) **Scope.** These rules of evidence govern proceedings in all courts of the Commonwealth of Pennsylvania's Unified Judicial System, except as otherwise provided by law.
(b) **Adoption and Citation.** These rules of evidence are adopted by the Supreme Court of Pennsylvania under the authority of Article V § 10(c) of the Constitution of Pennsylvania, adopted April 23, 1968. They shall be known as the Pennsylvania Rules of Evidence and shall be cited as "Pa.R.E."
(c) **Construction.** In the construction of the Pennsylvania Rules of Evidence, the principles set forth in Pa.R.J.A. 104 to 115 shall be observed.

Rule 102. Application of Rules.
These rules should be applied so as to administer every proceeding fairly, eliminate unjustifiable expense and delay, and promote the development of evidence law, to the end of ascertaining the truth and securing a just determination.

Rule 103. Rulings on Evidence
(a) **Preserving a Claim of Error.** A party may claim error in a ruling to admit or exclude evidence only:
    (1) if the ruling admits evidence, a party, on the record:
        (A) makes a timely objection, motion to strike, or motion *in limine*; and
        B) states the specific ground, unless it was apparent from the context; or
    (2) if the ruling excludes evidence, a party informs the court of its substance by an offer of proof, unless the substance was apparent from the context.
(b) **Not Needing to Renew an Objection or Offer of Proof.** Once the court rules definitively on the record--either before or at trial--a party need not renew an objection or offer of proof to preserve a claim of error for appeal.
(c) **Court's Statement About the Ruling; Directing an Offer of Proof.** The court may make any statement about the character or form of the evidence, the objection made, and the ruling. The court may direct that an offer of proof be made in question-and-answer form.
(d) **Preventing the Jury from Hearing Inadmissible Evidence.** To the extent practicable, the court must conduct a jury trial so that inadmissible evidence is not suggested to the jury by any means.

Rule 104. Preliminary Questions

(a) **In General.** The court must decide any preliminary question about whether a witness is qualified, a privilege exists, or evidence is admissible. In so deciding, the court is not bound by evidence rules, except those on privilege.

(b) **Relevance That Depends on a Fact.** When the relevance of evidence depends on whether a fact exists, proof must be introduced sufficient to support a finding that the fact does exist. The court may admit the proposed evidence on the condition that the proof be introduced later.

(c) **Conducting a Hearing So That the Jury Cannot Hear it.** The court must conduct any hearing on a preliminary question so that the jury cannot hear it if:

    (1) the hearing involves evidence alleged to have been obtained in violation of the defendant's rights;

    (2) a defendant in a criminal case is a witness and so requests; or

    (3) justice so requires.

(d) **Cross-Examining a Defendant in a Criminal Case.** By testifying on a preliminary question, a defendant in a criminal case does not become subject to cross-examination on other issues in the case.

(e) **Weight and Credibility.** Even though the court rules that evidence is admissible, this does not preclude a party from offering other evidence relevant to the weight or credibility of that evidence.

Rule 105. Limiting Evidence That is Not Admissible Against Other Parties or for Other Purposes

If the court admits evidence that is admissible against a party or for a purpose--but not against another party or for another purpose--the court, on timely request, must restrict the evidence to its proper scope and instruct the jury accordingly. The court may also do so on its own initiative.

Rule 106. Remainder of or Related Writings or Recorded Statements

If a party introduces all or part of a writing or recorded statement, an adverse party may require the introduction, at that time, of any other part--or any other writing or recorded statement--that in fairness ought to be considered at the same time.

ARTICLE II. JUDICIAL NOTICE

Rule 201. Judicial Notice of Adjudicative Facts
(a) **Scope.** This rule governs judicial notice of an adjudicative fact only, not a legislative fact.
(b) **Kinds of Facts That May Be Judicially Noticed.** The court may judicially notice a fact that is not subject to reasonable dispute because it:
    (1) is generally known within the trial court's territorial jurisdiction; or
    (2) can be accurately and readily determined from sources whose accuracy cannot reasonably be questioned.
(c) **Taking Notice.** The court:
    (1) may take judicial notice on its own; or
    (2) must take judicial notice if a party requests it and the court is supplied with the necessary information.
(d) **Timing.** The court may take judicial notice at any stage of the proceeding.
(e) **Opportunity to Be Heard.** On timely request, a party is entitled to be heard on the propriety of taking judicial notice and the nature of the fact to be noticed. If the court takes judicial notice before notifying a party, the party, on request, is still entitled to be heard.
(f) **Instructing the Jury.** The court must instruct the jury that it may, but is not required to, accept as conclusive any fact judicially noticed.

ARTICLE III. PRESUMPTIONS

Rule 301. Presumptions
Presumptions as they now exist or may be modified by law shall be unaffected by the adoption of these rules.

ARTICLE IV. RELEVANCE AND ITS LIMITS

Rule 401. Test for Relevant Evidence
Evidence is relevant if:
    (a) it has any tendency to make a fact more or less probable than it would be without the evidence; and
    (b) the fact is of consequence in determining the action.

Rule 402. General Admissibility of Relevant Evidence
All relevant evidence is admissible, except as otherwise provided by law. Evidence that is not relevant is not admissible.

Rule 403. Excluding Relevant Evidence for Prejudice, Confusion, Waste of Time, or Other Reasons
The court may exclude relevant evidence if its probative value is outweighed by a danger of one or more of the following: unfair prejudice, confusing the issues, misleading the jury, undue delay, wasting time, or needlessly presenting cumulative evidence.

Rule 404. Character Evidence; Other Crimes, Wrongs, or Acts

(a) **Character Evidence.**

(1) **Prohibited Uses.** Evidence of a person's character or character trait is not admissible to prove that on a particular occasion the person acted in accordance with the character or trait.

(2) **Exceptions for a Defendant or Victim in a Criminal Case.** The following exceptions apply in a criminal case:

(A) a defendant may offer evidence of the defendant's pertinent trait, and if the evidence is admitted, the prosecutor may offer evidence to rebut it;

(B) subject to limitations imposed by statute a defendant may offer evidence of an alleged victim's pertinent trait, and if the evidence is admitted the prosecutor may:

(i) offer evidence to rebut it; and

(ii) offer evidence of the defendant's same trait; and

(C) in a homicide case, the prosecutor may offer evidence of the alleged victim's trait of peacefulness to rebut evidence that the victim was the first aggressor.

(3) **Exceptions for a Witness.** Evidence of a witness's character may be admitted under Rules 607, 608, and 609.

(4) **Exception in a Civil Action for Assault and Battery.** In a civil action for assault and battery, evidence of the plaintiff's character trait for violence may be admitted when offered by the defendant to rebut evidence that the defendant was the first aggressor.

(b) **Other Crimes, Wrongs, or Acts.**

(1) **Prohibited Uses.** Evidence of any other crime, wrong, or act is not admissible to prove a person's character in order to show that on a particular occasion the person acted in accordance with the character.

(2) **Permitted Uses.** This evidence may be admissible for another purpose, such as proving motive, opportunity, intent, preparation, plan, knowledge, identity, absence of mistake, or lack of accident. In a criminal case this evidence is admissible only if the probative value of the evidence outweighs its potential for unfair prejudice.

(3) **Notice in a Criminal Case.** In a criminal case the prosecutor must provide reasonable written notice in advance of trial so that the defendant has a fair opportunity to meet it, or during trial if the court excuses pretrial notice on good cause shown, of the specific nature, permitted use, and reasoning for the use of any such evidence the prosecutor intends to introduce at trial.

Rule 405. Methods of Proving Character

(a) **By Reputation.** When evidence of a person's character or character trait is admissible, it may be proved by testimony about the person's reputation. Testimony about the witness's opinion as to the character or character trait of the person is not admissible.

(1) On cross-examination of the character witness, the court may allow an inquiry into relevant specific instances of the person's conduct probative of the character trait in question.

(2) In a criminal case, on cross-examination of a character witness, inquiry into allegations of other criminal conduct by the defendant, not resulting in conviction, is not permissible.

(b) **By Specific Instances of Conduct.** Specific instances of conduct are not admissible to prove character or a trait of character, except:

(1) In a civil case, when a person's character or a character trait is an essential element of a claim or defense, character may be proved by specific instances of conduct.

(2) In a criminal case, when character or a character trait of an alleged victim is admissible under Pa.R.E. 404(a)(2)(B) the defendant may prove the character or character trait by specific instances of conduct.

Rule 406. Habit; Routine Practice

Evidence of a person's habit or an organization's routine practice may be admitted to prove that on a particular occasion the person or organization acted in accordance with the habit or routine practice. The court may admit this evidence regardless of whether it is corroborated or there was an eyewitness.

Rule 407. Subsequent Remedial Measures
When measures are taken by a party that would have made an earlier injury or harm less likely to occur, evidence of the subsequent measures is not admissible against that party to prove:
- negligence;
- culpable conduct;
- a defect in a product or its design; or
- a need for a warning or instruction.

But the court may admit this evidence for another purpose such as impeachment or--if disputed--proving ownership, control, or the feasibility of precautionary measures.

Rule 408. Compromise Offers and Negotiations
(a) **Prohibited Uses.** Evidence of the following is not admissible--on behalf of any party--either to prove or disprove the validity or amount of a disputed claim or to impeach by a prior inconsistent statement or a contradiction:

(1) furnishing, promising, or offering--or accepting, promising to accept, or offering to accept--a valuable consideration in compromising or attempting to compromise the claim; and

(2) conduct or a statement made during compromise negotiations about the claim.

(b) **Exceptions.** The court may admit this evidence for another purpose, such as proving a witness's bias or prejudice, negating a contention of undue delay, or proving an effort to obstruct a criminal investigation or prosecution.

Rule 409. Offers to Pay Medical and Similar Expenses
Evidence of furnishing, promising to pay, or offering to pay medical, hospital, or similar expenses resulting from an injury is not admissible to prove liability for the injury.

Rule 410. Pleas, Plea Discussions, and Related Statements
(a) **Prohibited Uses.** In a civil or criminal case, evidence of the following is not admissible against the defendant who made the plea or participated in the plea discussions:
   (1) a guilty plea that was later withdrawn;
   (2) a nolo contendere plea;
   (3) a statement made in the course of any proceedings under Rules 311, 313, 409, 414, 424, 550 or 590 of the Pennsylvania Rules of Criminal Procedure, Rule 11 of the Federal Rules of Criminal Procedure, or a comparable rule or procedure of another state; or
   (4) a statement made during plea discussions with an attorney for the prosecuting authority if the discussions did not result in a guilty plea or they resulted in a later withdrawn guilty plea.
(b) **Exceptions.** The court may admit a statement described in Rule 410(a)(3) or (4):
   (1) in any proceeding in which another statement made during the same plea or plea discussions has been introduced, if in fairness the statements ought to be considered together; or
   (2) in a criminal proceeding for perjury, false swearing or unsworn falsification to authorities, if the defendant made the statement under oath, on the record, and with counsel present.

Rule 411. Liability Insurance
Evidence that a person was or was not insured against liability is not admissible to prove whether the person acted negligently or otherwise wrongfully. But the court may admit this evidence for another purpose, such as proving a witness's bias or prejudice or proving agency, ownership, or control.

Rule 412. Sex Offense Cases: The Victim's Sexual Behavior or Predisposition (Not Adopted)
But 18 Pa.C.S. § 3104 (the "Rape Shield Law").provides,
§ 3104. Evidence of victim's sexual conduct
(a) **General rule.**--Evidence of specific instances of the alleged victim's past sexual conduct, opinion evidence of the alleged victim's past sexual conduct, and reputation evidence of the alleged victim's past sexual conduct shall not be admissible in prosecutions under this chapter except evidence of the alleged victim's past sexual conduct with the defendant where consent of the alleged victim is at issue and such evidence is otherwise admissible pursuant to the rules of evidence.

(b) **Evidentiary proceedings.**--A defendant who proposes to offer evidence of the alleged victim's past sexual conduct pursuant to subsection (a) shall file a written motion and offer of proof at the time of trial. If, at the time of trial, the court determines that the motion and offer of proof are sufficient on their faces, the court shall order an in camera hearing and shall make findings on the record as to the relevance and admissibility of the proposed evidence pursuant to the standards set forth in subsection (a).

Rule 413. Evidence of Immigration Status.
(a) **Criminal or Delinquency Matters; Evidence Generally Inadmissible.** In any criminal or delinquency matter, evidence of a party's or a witness's immigration status shall not be admissible unless immigration status is an essential fact to prove an element of, or a defense to, the offense, to show motive, or to show bias or prejudice of a witness pursuant to Rule 607. This paragraph shall not be construed to exclude evidence that would result in the violation of a defendant's or a juvenile's constitutional rights.

(b) **Civil Matters; Evidence Generally Inadmissible**. In any civil matter, evidence of a party's or a witness's immigration status shall not be admissible unless immigration status is an essential fact to prove an element of, or a defense to, the action, or to show bias or prejudice of a witness pursuant to Rule 607.

(c) **Procedure**. Unless a party did not know, and with due diligence could not have known, that evidence of immigration status would be necessary, the following procedure shall apply prior to any such proposed use of immigration status evidence:

(1) The proponent shall file under seal and serve a written pretrial motion containing an offer of proof of the relevancy of the proposed evidence supported by an affidavit.

(2) If the court finds that the offer of proof is sufficient, the court shall order an in camera hearing.

(3) The court may admit evidence of immigration status pursuant to paragraph (a) or paragraph (b) if it finds the evidence is reliable and relevant, and that its probative value outweighs the prejudicial nature of evidence of immigration status.

(d) **Voluntary Revelation.** This rule shall not prohibit a person, or the person's attorney, from voluntarily revealing his or her immigration status to the court.

ARTICLE V. PRIVILEGES

Rule 501. Privileges
Privileges as they now exist or may be modified by law shall be unaffected by the adoption of these rules.

Rule 502. Attorney-Client Privilege and Work Product; Limitations on Waiver (Not Adopted)

ARTICLE VI. WITNESSES

Rule 601. Competency
(a) **General Rule.** Every person is competent to be a witness except as otherwise provided by statute or in these rules.
(b) **Disqualification for Specific Defects.** A person is incompetent to testify if the court finds that because of a mental condition or immaturity the person:
    (1) is, or was, at any relevant time, incapable of perceiving accurately;
    (2) is unable to express himself or herself so as to be understood either directly or through an interpreter;
    (3) has an impaired memory; or
    (4) does not sufficiently understand the duty to tell the truth.

Rule 602. Need for Personal Knowledge
A witness may testify to a matter only if evidence is introduced sufficient to support a finding that the witness has personal knowledge of the matter. Evidence to prove personal knowledge may consist of the witness's own testimony. This rule does not apply to a witness's expert testimony under Rule 703.

Rule 603. Oath or Affirmation to Testify Truthfully
Before testifying, a witness must give an oath or affirmation to testify truthfully. It must be in a form designed to impress that duty on the witness's conscience.

Rule 604. Interpreter
An interpreter must be qualified and must give an oath or affirmation to make a true translation.

Rule 605. Judge's Competency as a Witness
The presiding judge may not testify as a witness at the trial or other proceeding.

Rule 606. Juror's Competency as a Witness

(a) **At the Trial.** A juror may not testify as a witness before the other jurors at the trial. If a juror is called to testify, the court must give a party an opportunity to object outside the jury's presence.

(b) **During an Inquiry into the Validity of a Verdict**

(1) **Prohibited Testimony or Other Evidence.** During an inquiry into the validity of a verdict, a juror may not testify about any statement made or incident that occurred during the jury's deliberations; the effect of anything on that juror's or another juror's vote; or any juror's mental processes concerning the verdict. The court may not receive a juror's affidavit or evidence of a juror's statement on these matters.

(2) **Exceptions.** A juror may testify about whether:

(A) prejudicial information not of record and beyond common knowledge and experience was improperly brought to the jury's attention; or

(B) an outside influence was improperly brought to bear on any juror.

Rule 607. Who May Impeach a Witness, Evidence to Impeach a Witness

(a) **Who May Impeach a Witness.** Any party, including the party that called the witness, may attack the witness's credibility.

(b) **Evidence to Impeach a Witness.** The credibility of a witness may be impeached by any evidence relevant to that issue, except as otherwise provided by statute or these rules.

Rule 608. A Witness's Character for Truthfulness or Untruthfulness

(a) **Reputation Evidence.** A witness's credibility may be attacked or supported by testimony about the witness's reputation for having a character for truthfulness or untruthfulness. But evidence of truthful character is admissible only after the witness's character for truthfulness has been attacked. Opinion testimony about the witness's character for truthfulness or untruthfulness is not admissible.

(b) **Specific Instances of Conduct.** Except as provided in Rule 609 (relating to evidence of conviction of crime),

(1) the character of a witness for truthfulness may not be attacked or supported by cross-examination or extrinsic evidence concerning specific instances of the witness' conduct; however,

(2) in the discretion of the court, the credibility of a witness who testifies as to the reputation of another witness for truthfulness or untruthfulness may be attacked by cross-examination concerning specific instances of conduct (not including arrests) of the other witness, if they are probative of truthfulness or untruthfulness; but extrinsic evidence thereof is not admissible.

Rule 609. Impeachment by Evidence of a Criminal Conviction

(a) **In General.** For the purpose of attacking the credibility of any witness, evidence that the witness has been convicted of a crime, whether by verdict or by plea of guilty or nolo contendere, must be admitted if it involved dishonesty or false statement.

(b) **Limit on Using the Evidence After 10 Years.** This subdivision (b) applies if more than 10 years have passed since the witness's conviction or release from confinement for it, whichever is later. Evidence of the conviction is admissible only if:

    (1) its probative value substantially outweighs its prejudicial effect; and

    (2) the proponent gives an adverse party reasonable written notice of the intent to use it so that the party has a fair opportunity to contest its use.

(c) **Effect of Pardon or Other Equivalent Procedure.** Evidence of a conviction is not admissible under this rule if the conviction has been the subject of one of the following:

    (1) a pardon or other equivalent procedure based on a specific finding of innocence; or

    (2) a pardon or other equivalent procedure based on a specific finding of rehabilitation of the person convicted, and that person has not been convicted of any subsequent crime.

(d) **Juvenile Adjudications.** In a criminal case only, evidence of the adjudication of delinquency for an offense under the Juvenile Act, 42 Pa.C.S. §§ 6301 *et seq.*, may be used to impeach the credibility of a witness if conviction of the offense would be admissible to attack the credibility of an adult.

(e) **Pendency of an Appeal.** A conviction that satisfies this rule is admissible even if an appeal is pending. Evidence of the pendency is also admissible.

Rule 610. Religious Beliefs or Opinions

Evidence of a witness's religious beliefs or opinions is not admissible to attack or support the witness's credibility.

Rule 611. Mode and Order of Examining Witnesses and Presenting Evidence

(a) **Control by the Court; Purposes.** The court should exercise reasonable control over the mode and order of examining witnesses and presenting evidence so as to:
    (1) make those procedures effective for determining the truth;
    (2) avoid wasting time; and
    (3) protect witnesses from harassment or undue embarrassment.

(b) **Scope of Cross-Examination.** Cross-examination of a witness other than a party in a civil case should be limited to the subject matter of the direct examination and matters affecting credibility, however, the court may, in the exercise of discretion, permit inquiry into additional matters as if on direct examination. A party witness in a civil case may be cross-examined by an adverse party on any matter relevant to any issue in the case, including credibility, unless the court, in the interests of justice, limits the cross-examination with respect to matters not testified to on direct examination.

(c) **Leading Questions.** Leading questions should not be used on direct or redirect examination except as necessary to develop the witness's testimony. Ordinarily, the court should allow leading questions:
    (1) on cross-examination; and
    (2) when a party calls a hostile witness, an adverse party, or a witness identified with an adverse party. A witness so examined should usually be interrogated by all other parties as to whom the witness is not hostile or adverse as if under redirect examination.

Rule 612. Writing or Other Item Used to Refresh a Witness's Memory

(a) **Right to Refresh Memory.** A witness may use a writing or other item to refresh memory for the purpose of testifying while testifying, or before testifying.

(b) **Rights of Adverse Party.**

(1) If a witness uses a writing or other item to refresh memory while testifying, an adverse party is entitled to have it produced at the hearing, trial or deposition, to inspect it, to cross-examine the witness about it, and to introduce in evidence any portion that relates to the witness's testimony.

(2) If a witness uses a writing or other item to refresh memory before testifying, and the court in its discretion determines it is necessary in the interests of justice, an adverse party is entitled to have it produced at the hearing, trial or deposition, to inspect it, to cross-examine the witness about it, and to introduce in evidence any portion that relates to the witness's testimony.

(c) **Rights of Producing Party.** If the producing party claims that the writing or other item includes unrelated matter, the court must examine it in camera, delete any unrelated portion, and order that the rest be delivered to the adverse party. Any portion deleted over objection must be preserved for the record.

(d) **Failure to Produce or Deliver.** If the writing or other item is not produced or is not delivered as ordered, the court may issue any appropriate order. But if the prosecution does not comply in a criminal case, the court must strike the witness's testimony or--if justice so requires--declare a mistrial, or the court may use contempt procedures.

Rule 613. Witness's Prior Inconsistent Statement to Impeach; Witness's Prior Consistent Statement to Rehabilitate

(a) **Witness's Prior Inconsistent Statement to Impeach.** A witness may be examined concerning a prior inconsistent statement made by the witness to impeach the witness's credibility. The statement need not be shown or its contents disclosed to the witness at that time, but on request, the statement or contents must be shown or disclosed to an adverse party's attorney.

(b) **Extrinsic Evidence of a Witness's Prior Inconsistent Statement.** Unless the interests of justice otherwise require, extrinsic evidence of a witness's prior inconsistent statement is admissible only if, during the examination of the witness,

(1) the statement, if written, is shown to, or if not written, its contents are disclosed to, the witness;

(2) the witness is given an opportunity to explain or deny the making of the statement; and

(3) an adverse party is given an opportunity to question the witness.

This paragraph does not apply to an opposing party's statement as defined in Rule 803(25).

(c) **Witness's Prior Consistent Statement to Rehabilitate.** Evidence of a witness's prior consistent statement is admissible to rehabilitate the witness's credibility if the opposing party is given an opportunity to cross-examine the witness about the statement and the statement is offered to rebut an express or implied charge of:

(1) fabrication, bias, improper influence or motive, or faulty memory and the statement was made before that which has been charged existed or arose; or

(2) having made a prior inconsistent statement, which the witness has denied or explained, and the consistent statement supports the witness's denial or explanation.

Rule 614. Court's Calling or Examining a Witness

(a) Calling. Consistent with its function as an impartial arbiter, the court, with notice to the parties, may call a witness on its own or at a party's request. Each party is entitled to cross-examine the witness.

(b) Examining. Where the interest of justice so requires, the court may examine a witness regardless of who calls the witness.

(c) Objections. A party may object to the court's calling or examining a witness when given notice that the witness will be called or when the witness is examined. When requested to do so, the court must give the objecting party an opportunity to make objections out of the presence of the jury.

Rule 615. Sequestering Witnesses

At a party's request the court may order witnesses sequestered so that they cannot learn of other witnesses' testimony. Or the court may do so on its own. But this rule does not authorize sequestering:

    (a) a party who is a natural person;
    (b) an officer or employee of a party that is not a natural person (including the Commonwealth) after being designated as the party's representative by its attorney;
    (c) a person whose presence a party shows to be essential to presenting the party's claim or defense; or
    (d) a person authorized by statute or rule to be present.

ARTICLE VII. Opinions and Expert Testimony

Rule 701. Opinion Testimony by Lay Witnesses
If a witness is not testifying as an expert, testimony in the form of an opinion is limited to one that is:
    (a) rationally based on the witness's perception;
    (b) helpful to clearly understanding the witness's testimony or to determining a fact in issue; and
    (c) not based on scientific, technical, or other specialized knowledge within the scope of Rule 702.

Rule 702. Testimony by Expert Witnesses
A witness who is qualified as an expert by knowledge, skill, experience, training, or education may testify in the form of an opinion or otherwise if:
    (a) the expert's scientific, technical, or other specialized knowledge is beyond that possessed by the average layperson;
    (b) the expert's scientific, technical, or other specialized knowledge will help the trier of fact to understand the evidence or to determine a fact in issue; and
    (c) the expert's methodology is generally accepted in the relevant field.

Rule 703. Bases of an Expert's Opinion Testimony
An expert may base an opinion on facts or data in the case that the expert has been made aware of or personally observed. If experts in the particular field would reasonably rely on those kinds of facts or data in forming an opinion on the subject, they need not be admissible for the opinion to be admitted.

Rule 704. Opinion on an Ultimate Issue
An opinion is not objectionable just because it embraces an ultimate issue.

Rule 705. Disclosing the Facts or Data Underlying an Expert's Opinion
If an expert states an opinion the expert must state the facts or data on which the opinion is based.

Rule 706. Court-Appointed Expert Witnesses
Where the court has appointed an expert witness, the witness appointed must advise the parties of the witness's findings, if any. The witness may be called to testify by the court or any party. The witness shall be subject to cross-examination by any party, including a party calling the witness. In civil cases, the witness's deposition may be taken by any party.

ARTICLE VIII. HEARSAY

Rule 801. Definitions That Apply to This Article

(a) **Statement.** "Statement" means a person's oral assertion, written assertion, or nonverbal conduct, if the person intended it as an assertion.

(b) **Declarant.** "Declarant" means the person who made the statement.

(c) **Hearsay.** "Hearsay" means a statement that
   (1) the declarant does not make while testifying at the current trial or hearing; and
   (2) a party offers in evidence to prove the truth of the matter asserted in the statement.

Rule 802. The Rule Against Hearsay

Hearsay is not admissible except as provided by these rules, by other rules prescribed by the Pennsylvania Supreme Court, or by statute.

Rule 803. Exceptions to the Rule Against Hearsay-- Regardless of Whether the Declarant Is Available as a Witness

The following are not excluded by the rule against hearsay, regardless of whether the declarant is available as a witness:

   (1) **Present Sense Impression.** A statement describing or explaining an event or condition, made while or immediately after the declarant perceived it. When the declarant is unidentified, the proponent shall show by independent corroborating evidence that the declarant actually perceived the event or condition.

   (2) **Excited Utterance.** A statement relating to a startling event or condition, made while the declarant was under the stress of excitement that it caused. When the declarant is unidentified, the proponent shall show by independent corroborating evidence that the declarant actually perceived the startling event or condition.

Rule 803(3). Then-Existing Mental, Emotional, or Physical Condition

(3) **Then-Existing Mental, Emotional, or Physical Condition.** A statement of the declarant's then-existing state of mind (such as motive, intent or plan) or emotional, sensory, or physical condition (such as mental feeling, pain, or bodily health), but not including a statement of memory or belief to prove the fact remembered or believed unless it relates to the validity or terms of the declarant's will.

(4) **Statement Made for Medical Diagnosis or Treatment.** A statement that:

(5) **Recorded Recollection** (Not Adopted in this position of the rules but see it as Rule. 803.1(3).)

(6) **Records of a Regularly Conducted Activity.** A record (which includes a memorandum, report, or data compilation in any form) of an act, event or condition if:

> (A) the record was made at or near the time by--or from information transmitted by--someone with knowledge;
>
> (B) the record was kept in the course of a regularly conducted activity of a "business", which term includes business, institution, association, profession, occupation, and calling of every kind, whether or not conducted for profit;
>
> (C) making the record was a regular practice of that activity;
>
> (D) all these conditions are shown by the testimony of the custodian or another qualified witness, or by a certification that complies with Rule 902(11) or (12) or with a statute permitting certification; and
>
> (E) the <u>opponent does not show</u> that the source of information or other circumstances indicate a lack of trustworthiness.

(7) **Absence of a Record of a Regularly Conducted Activity** (Not Adopted – Author's Note: but still admissible says the comment to this rule because, "The absence of an entry in a record is not hearsay, as defined in Pa.R.E. 801(c). Hence, it appears irrational to except it to the hearsay rule... On analysis, absence of an entry in a business record is circumstantial evidence - it tends to prove something by implication, not assertion. Its admissibility is governed by principles of relevance, not hearsay. See Pa.R.E. 401, et seq.")

(8) **Public Records.** A record of a public office if:
   (A) the record describes the facts of the action taken or matter observed;
   (B) the recording of this action or matter observed was an official public duty; and
   (C) the <u>opponent does not show</u> that the source of the information or other circumstances indicate a lack of trustworthiness.

(9) **Public Records of Vital Statistics** (Not Adopted – Author's Note: but still admissible says the comment to this rule because records of vital statistics are also records of a regularly conducted activity and therefore exceptions to the hearsay rule by Pa.R.E. 803(6). Records of vital statistics are public records and they may be excepted to the hearsay rule by 42 Pa.C.S. § 6104. See also 35 P.S. § 450.101 et seq. and 35 P.S. § 450.810.)

(10) **Non-Existence of a Public Record.** Testimony--or a certification--that a diligent search failed to disclose a public record if:
   (A) the testimony or certification is admitted to prove that
      (i) the record does not exist; or
      (ii) a matter did not occur or exist, if a public office regularly kept a record for a matter of that kind.
   (B) in a criminal case:
      (i) the attorney for the Commonwealth who intends to offer a certification files and serves written notice of that intent upon the defendant's attorney or, if unrepresented, the defendant, at least 20 days before trial; and
      (ii) defendant's attorney or, if unrepresented, the defendant, does not file and serve a written demand for testimony in lieu of the certification within 10 days of service of the notice.

(11) **Records of Religious Organizations Concerning Personal or Family History.** A statement of birth, legitimacy, ancestry, marriage, divorce, death, relationship by blood or marriage, or similar facts of personal or family history, contained in a regularly kept record of a religious organization.

(12) **Certificates of Marriage, Baptism, and Similar Ceremonies.** A statement of fact contained in a certificate:
   (A) made by a person who is authorized by a religious organization or by law to perform the act certified;
   (B) attesting that the person performed a marriage or similar ceremony or administered a sacrament; and
   (C) purporting to have been issued at the time of the act or within a reasonable time after it.

(13) **Family Records.** A statement of fact about personal or family history contained in a family record, such as a Bible, genealogy, chart, engraving on a ring, inscription on a portrait, or engraving on an urn or burial marker.

(14) **Records of Documents That Affect an Interest in Property.** The record of a document that purports to establish or affect an interest in property if:
   (A) the record is admitted to prove the content of the original recorded document, along with its signing and its delivery by each person who purports to have signed it;
   (B) the record is kept in a public office; and
   (C) a statute authorizes recording documents of that kind in that office.

(15) **Statements in Documents That Affect an Interest in Property.** A statement contained in a document, other than a will, that purports to establish or affect an interest in property if the matter stated was relevant to the document's purpose--unless later dealings with the property are inconsistent with the truth of the statement or the purport of the document.

(16) **Statements in Ancient Documents.** A statement in a document that is at least 30 years old and whose authenticity is established.

(17) **Market Reports and Similar Commercial Publications.** Market quotations, lists, directories, or other compilations that are generally relied on by the public or by persons in particular occupations.

(18) **Statements in Learned Treatises, Periodicals, or Pamphlets** (Not Adopted – See Majdic v. Cincinnati Machine Co., 370 Pa. Super. 611, 537 A.2d 334 (1988).

(19) Reputation Concerning Personal or Family History. A reputation among a person's family by blood, adoption, or marriage--or among a person's associates or in the community--concerning the person's birth, adoption, legitimacy, ancestry, marriage, divorce, death, relationship by blood, adoption, or marriage, or similar facts of personal or family history.

(20) Reputation Concerning Boundaries or General History. A reputation in a community--arising before the controversy--concerning boundaries of land in the community or customs that affect the land, or concerning general historical events important to that community, state or nation.

(21) Reputation Concerning Character. A reputation among a person's associates or in the community concerning the person's character.

(22) Judgment of a Previous Conviction (Not Adopted)

(23) Judgments Involving Personal, Family, or General History or a Boundary (Not Adopted)

(24) Other Exceptions (Not Adopted)

(25) An Opposing Party's Statement. The statement is offered against an opposing party and:
   (A) was made by the party in an individual or representative capacity;
   (B) is one the party manifested that it adopted or believed to be true;
   (C) was made by a person whom the party authorized to make a statement on the subject;
   (D) was made by the party's agent or employee on a matter within the scope of that relationship and while it existed; or
   (E) was made by the party's coconspirator during and in furtherance of the conspiracy.

The statement may be considered but does not by itself establish the declarant's authority under (C); the existence or scope of the relationship under (D); or the existence of the conspiracy or participation in it under (E).

Rule 803.1. Exceptions to the Rule Against Hearsay-- Testimony of Declarant Necessary

The following statements are not excluded by the rule against hearsay if the declarant testifies and is subject to cross-examination about the prior statement:

(1) **Prior Inconsistent Statement of Declarant-Witness.** A prior statement by a declarant-witness that is inconsistent with the declarant-witness's testimony and:

(A) was given under oath subject to the penalty of perjury at a trial, hearing, or other proceeding, or in a deposition;

(B) is a writing signed and adopted by the declarant; or

(C) is a verbatim contemporaneous electronic recording of an oral statement.

(2) **Prior Statement of Identification by Declarant-Witness.** A prior statement by a declarant-witness identifying a person or thing, made after perceiving the person or thing, provided that the declarant-witness testifies to the making of the prior statement.

(3) **Recorded Recollection of Declarant-Witness.** A memorandum or record made or adopted by a declarant-witness that:

(A) is on a matter the declarant-witness once knew about but now cannot recall well enough to testify fully and accurately;

(B) was made or adopted by the declarant-witness when the matter was fresh in his or her memory; and

(C) the declarant-witness testifies accurately reflects his or her knowledge at the time when made.

If admitted, the memorandum or record may be read into evidence and received as an exhibit, but may be shown to the jury only in exceptional circumstances or when offered by an adverse party.

(4) Prior Statement by a Declarant-Witness Who Claims an Inability to Remember the Subject Matter of the Statement. A prior statement by a declarant-witness who testifies to an inability to remember the subject matter of the statement, unless the court finds the claimed inability to remember to be credible, and the statement:
    (A) was given under oath subject to the penalty of perjury at a trial, hearing, or other proceeding, or in a deposition;
    (B) is a writing signed and adopted by the declarant; or
    (C) is a verbatim contemporaneous electronic recording of an oral statement.

Rule 804. Exceptions to the Rule Against Hearsay--When the Declarant is Unavailable as a Witness
    (a) **Criteria for Being Unavailable.** A declarant is considered to be unavailable as a witness if the declarant:
        (1) is exempted from testifying about the subject matter of the declarant's statement because the court rules that a privilege applies;
        (2) refuses to testify about the subject matter despite a court order to do so;
        (3) testifies to not remembering the subject matter, except as provided in Rule 803.1(4);
        (4) cannot be present or testify at the trial or hearing because of death or a then-existing infirmity, physical illness, or mental illness; or
        (5) is absent from the trial or hearing and the statement's proponent has not been able, by process or other reasonable means, to procure:
            (A) the declarant's attendance, in the case of a hearsay exception under Rule 804(b)(1) or (6); or
            (B) the declarant's attendance or testimony, in the case of a hearsay exception under Rule 804(b)(2), (3), or (4).
    But this paragraph (a) does not apply if the statement's proponent procured or wrongfully caused the declarant's unavailability as a witness in order to prevent the declarant from attending or testifying.

Rule 804(b). Exceptions to the Rule Against Hearsay--When the Declarant is Unavailable as a Witness

(b) **The Exceptions.** The following are not excluded by the rule against hearsay if the declarant is unavailable as a witness:
- (1) **Former Testimony.** Testimony that:
    - (A) was given as a witness at a trial, hearing, or lawful deposition, whether given during the current proceeding or a different one; and
    - (B) is now offered against a party who had--or, in a civil case, whose predecessor in interest had--an opportunity and similar motive to develop it by direct, cross-, or redirect examination.
- (2) **Statement Under Belief of Imminent Death.** A statement that the declarant, while believing the declarant's death to be imminent, made about its cause or circumstances.
- (3) **Statement Against Interest.** A statement that:
    - (A) a reasonable person in the declarant's position would have made only if the person believed it to be true because, when made, it was so contrary to the declarant's proprietary or pecuniary interest or had so great a tendency to invalidate the declarant's claim against someone else or to expose the declarant to civil or criminal liability; and
    - (B) is supported by corroborating circumstances that clearly indicate its trustworthiness, if it is offered in a criminal case as one that tends to expose the declarant to criminal liability.
- (4) **Statement of Personal or Family History.** A statement made before the controversy arose about:
    - (A) the declarant's own birth, adoption, legitimacy, ancestry, marriage, divorce, relationship by blood, adoption or marriage, or similar facts of personal or family history, even though the declarant had no way of acquiring personal knowledge about that fact; or
    - (B) another person concerning any of these facts, as well as death, if the declarant was related to the person by blood, adoption, or marriage or was so intimately associated with the person's family that the declarant's information is likely to be accurate.
- (5) **Other exceptions** (Not Adopted)

(6) Statement Offered Against a Party That Wrongfully Caused the Declarant's Unavailability. A statement offered against a party that wrongfully caused--or acquiesced in wrongfully causing--the declarant's unavailability as a witness, and did so intending that result.

Rule 805. Hearsay Within Hearsay
Hearsay within hearsay is not excluded by the rule against hearsay if each part of the combined statements conforms with an exception to the rule.

Rule 806. Attacking and Supporting the Declarant's Credibility
When a hearsay statement has been admitted in evidence, the declarant's credibility may be attacked, and then supported, by any evidence that would be admissible for those purposes if the declarant had testified as a witness. The court may admit evidence of the declarant's inconsistent statement or conduct, regardless of when it occurred or whether the declarant had an opportunity to explain or deny it. If the party against whom the statement was admitted calls the declarant as a witness, the party may examine the declarant on the statement as if on cross-examination.

Rule 807. Residual Exception (Not Adopted)

ARTICLE IX. AUTHENTICATION AND IDENTIFICATION

Rule 901. Authenticating or Identifying Evidence
(a) **In General.** Unless stipulated, to satisfy the requirement of authenticating or identifying an item of evidence, the proponent must produce evidence sufficient to support a finding that the item is what the proponent claims it is.
(b) **Examples.** The following are examples only--not a complete list--of evidence that satisfies the requirement:
    (1) **Testimony of a Witness with Knowledge.** Testimony that an item is what it is claimed to be.

Rule 901(b)(2). Nonexpert Opinion about Handwriting.

(2) **Nonexpert Opinion about Handwriting.** A nonexpert's opinion that handwriting is genuine, based on a familiarity with it that was not acquired for the current litigation.

(3) **Comparison by an Expert Witness or the Trier of Fact.** A comparison with an authenticated specimen by an expert witness or the trier of fact.

(4) **Distinctive Characteristics and the Like.** The appearance, contents, substance, internal patterns, or other distinctive characteristics of the item, taken together with all the circumstances.

(5) **Opinion About a Voice.** An opinion identifying a person's voice--whether heard firsthand or through mechanical or electronic transmission or recording--based on hearing the voice at any time under circumstances that connect it with the alleged speaker.

(6) **Evidence About a Telephone Conversation.** For a telephone conversation, evidence that a call was made to the number assigned at the time to:

    (A) a particular person, if circumstances, including self-identification, show that the person answering was the one called; or

    (B) a particular business, if the call was made to a business and the call related to business reasonably transacted over the telephone.

(7) **Evidence About Public Records.** Evidence that:

    (A) a document was recorded or filed in a public office as authorized by law; or

    (B) a purported public record or statement is from the office where items of this kind are kept.

(8) **Evidence About Ancient Documents or Data Compilations.** For a document or data compilation, evidence that it:

    (A) is in a condition that creates no suspicion about its authenticity;

    (B) was in a place where, if authentic, it would likely be; and

    (C) is at least 30 years old when offered.

(9) **Evidence About a Process or System.** Evidence describing a process or system and showing that it produces an accurate result.

(10) **Methods Provided by a Statute or a Rule.** Any method of authentication or identification allowed by a statute or a rule prescribed by the Supreme Court.

(11) **Digital Evidence.** To connect digital evidence with a person or entity:

    (A) direct evidence such as testimony of a person with personal knowledge; or

    (B) circumstantial evidence such as:

        (i) identifying content; or

        (ii) proof of ownership, possession, control, or access to a device or account at the relevant time when corroborated by circumstances indicating authorship.

Rule 902. Evidence That is Self-Authenticating
The following items of evidence are self-authenticating; they require no extrinsic evidence of authenticity in order to be admitted:

(1) **Domestic Public Documents That Are Sealed and Signed.** A document that bears:

   (A) a seal purporting to be that of the United States; any state, district, commonwealth, territory, or insular possession of the United States; the former Panama Canal Zone; the Trust Territory of the Pacific Islands; a political subdivision of any of these entities; or a department, agency, or officer of any entity named above; and
   (B) a signature purporting to be an execution or attestation.

(2) **Domestic Public Documents That Are Not Sealed but Are Signed and Certified.** A document that bears no seal if:

   (A) it bears the signature of an officer or employee of an entity named in Rule 902(1)(A); and
   (B) another public officer who has a seal and official duties within that same entity certifies under seal--or its equivalent--that the signer has the official capacity and that the signature is genuine.

(3) **Foreign Public Documents.** A document that purports to be signed or attested by a person who is authorized by a foreign country's law to do so. The document must be accompanied by a final certification that certifies the genuineness of the signature and official position of the signer or attester--or of any foreign official whose certificate of genuineness relates to the signature or attestation or is in a chain of certificates of genuineness relating to the signature or attestation. The certification may be made by a secretary of a United States embassy or legation; by a consul general, vice consul, or consular agent of the United States; or by a diplomatic or consular official of the foreign country assigned or accredited to the United States. If all parties have been given a reasonable opportunity to investigate the document's authenticity and accuracy, the court may for good cause, either:

Rule 902(4). Certified Copies of Public Records

(A) order that it be treated as presumptively authentic without final certification; or

(B) allow it to be evidenced by an attested summary with or without final certification.

(4) Certified Copies of Public Records. A copy of an official record--or a copy of a document that was recorded or filed in a public office as authorized by law- if the copy is certified as correct by:

(A) the custodian or another person authorized to make the certification; or

(B) a certificate that complies with Rule 902(1), (2), or (3), a statute or a rule prescribed by the Supreme Court.

A certificate required by paragraph (4)(B) may include a handwritten signature, a copy of a handwritten signature, a computer generated signature, or a signature created, transmitted, received, or stored by electronic means, by the signer or by someone with the signer's authorization. A seal may, but need not, be raised.

(5) Official Publications. A book, pamphlet, or other publication purporting to be issued by a public authority.

(6) Newspapers and Periodicals. Material purporting to be a newspaper or periodical.

(7) Trade Inscriptions and the Like. An inscription, sign, tag, or label purporting to have been affixed in the course of business and indicating origin, ownership, or control.

(8) Acknowledged Documents. A document accompanied by a certificate of acknowledgment that is lawfully executed by a notary public or another officer who is authorized to take acknowledgments.

(9) Commercial Paper and Related Documents. Commercial paper, a signature on it, and related documents, to the extent allowed by general commercial law.

(10) Presumptions Authorized by Statute. A signature, document, or anything else that a statute declares to be presumptively or *prima facie* genuine or authentic.

(11) **Certified Domestic Records of a Regularly Conducted Activity.** The original or a copy of a domestic record that meets the requirements of Rule 803(6)(A)-(C), as shown by a certification of the custodian or another qualified person that complies with Pa.R.C.P. No. 76. Before the trial or hearing, the proponent must give an adverse party reasonable written notice of the intent to offer the record--and must make the record and certification available for inspection--so that the party has a fair opportunity to challenge them.

(12) **Certified Foreign Records of a Regularly Conducted Activity.** The original or a copy of a foreign record that meets the requirements of Rule 902(11), modified as follows: the certification rather than complying with a statute or Supreme Court rule, must be signed in a manner that, if falsely made, would subject the maker to a criminal penalty in the country where the certification is signed. The proponent must also meet the notice requirements of Rule 902(11).

(13) **Certified Records Generated by an Electronic Process or System.** A record generated by an electronic process or system that produces an accurate result, as shown by a certification of a qualified person that complies with the certification requirements of Rule 902(11) or (12). The proponent must also meet the notice requirements of Rule 902(11).

(14) **Certified Data Copied from an Electronic Device, Storage Medium, or File.** Data copied from an electronic device, storage medium, or file, if authenticated by a process of digital identification, as shown by a certification of a qualified person that complies with the certification requirements of Rule 902(11) or (12). The proponent also must meet the notice requirements of Rule 902(11).

(15) **Certificate of Non-Existence of a Public Record.** A certificate that a document was not recorded or filed in a public office as authorized by law if certified by the custodian or another person authorized to make the certificate.

Rule 903. Subscribing Witness's Testimony

A subscribing witness's testimony is necessary to authenticate a writing only if required by the law of the jurisdiction that governs its validity.

ARTICLE X. CONTENTS OF WRITINGS, RECORDINGS, AND PHOTOGRAPHS

Rule 1001. Definitions That Apply to This Article
In this article:
    (a) A "writing" consists of letters, words, numbers, or their equivalent set down in any form.
    (b) A "recording" consists of letters, words, numbers, or their equivalent recorded in any manner.
    (c) A "photograph" means a photographic image or its equivalent stored in any form.
    (d) An "original" of a writing or recording means the writing or recording itself or any counterpart intended to have the same effect by the person who executed or issued it. For electronically stored information, "original" means any printout--or other output readable by sight--if it accurately reflects the information. An "original" of a photograph includes the negative or a print from it.
    (e) A "duplicate" means a copy produced by a mechanical, photographic, chemical, electronic, or other equivalent process or technique that accurately reproduces the original.

Rule 1002. Requirement of the Original
An original writing, recording, or photograph is required in order to prove its content unless these rules, other rules prescribed by the Supreme Court, or a statute provides otherwise.

Rule 1003. Admissibility of Duplicates
A duplicate is admissible to the same extent as the original unless a genuine question is raised about the original's authenticity or the circumstances make it unfair to admit the duplicate.

Rule 1004. Admissibility of Other Evidence of Content
An original is not required and other evidence of the content of a writing, recording, or photograph is admissible if:
    (a) all the originals are lost or destroyed, and not by the proponent acting in bad faith;
    (b) an original cannot be obtained by any available judicial process;
    (c) the party against whom the original would be offered had control of the original; was at that time put on notice, by

pleadings or otherwise, that the original would be a subject of proof at the trial or hearing; and fails to produce it at the trial or hearing; or
(d) the writing, recording, or photograph is not closely related to a controlling issue.

Rule 1005. Copies of Public Records to Prove Content
The proponent may use a copy to prove the content of an official record--or of a document that was recorded or filed in a public office as authorized by law--if these conditions are met: the record or document is otherwise admissible; and the copy is certified as correct in accordance with Rule 902(4) or is testified to be correct by a witness who has compared it with the original. If no such copy can be obtained by reasonable diligence, then the proponent may use other evidence to prove the content.

Rule 1006. Summaries to Prove Content
The proponent may use a summary, chart, or calculation to prove the content of voluminous writings, recordings, or photographs that cannot be conveniently examined in court. The proponent must make the originals or duplicates available for examination or copying, or both, by other parties at a reasonable time and place. And the court may order the proponent to produce them in court.

Rule 1007. Testimony or Statement of a Party to Prove Content
The proponent may prove the content of a writing, recording, or photograph by the testimony, deposition, or written statement of the party against whom the evidence is offered. The proponent need not account for the original.

Rule 1008. Functions of the Court and Jury
Ordinarily, the court determines whether the proponent has fulfilled the factual conditions for admitting other evidence of the content of a writing, recording, or photograph under Rule 1004 or 1005. But in a jury trial, the jury determines--in accordance with Rule 104(b)--any issue about whether:
(a) an asserted writing, recording, or photograph ever existed;
(b) another one produced at the trial or hearing is the original; or
(c) other evidence of content accurately reflects the content.

Making and Responding to Common Objections

Professor John Barkai

> This section of the handbook provides ideas about making and responding to common objections, and it also includes a list of common objections.

There is almost an endless number of objections that could be made at a trial. There are many lists or "cheat sheets" of objections that can be found on the Internet and many articles about objections. This section of the handbook will discuss the basics about objections and provide a list of the more common objections.

Why Do Lawyers Object?
Lawyers object during trial to:

1) control the information that the fact finder can consider
   (to exclude testimony or exhibits offered by the opposing party),

2) control the opposing lawyer's conduct
   (to prevent certain questions or answers, prevent the calling of certain witnesses, prevent certain statements from being made during opening statements or closing arguments),

3) preserve errors for appeal,

4) disrupt opponent's counsel's momentum,

5) send a signal to a witness,

6) communicate with the fact finder, and

7) give the witness a break and time to think.

Lawyers frequently object to the form of question (Argumentative, Ambiguous, Vague, Asked and Answered, etc.) to prevent the judge or jury from hearing inadmissible evidence. Often, however, such objections are made simply to harass, annoy, upset, or distract opposing counsel. The less experience the lawyer doing trials has, the more such objections are likely to distract them. Some people consider objections made for such purposes to be "unethical;" other people consider such objections part of the competition in the adversary system. Whatever your view, be ready for such objections.

Make an Objection in Four Steps
1) Stand up.
2) Say, "Objection ____" (Fill in the blank with your reason).
3) Identify your specific objection.
   a) At a minimum, say the topic type
      (Hearsay, Relevance, Improper Impeachment, Improper Character, Lack of Foundation, Leading Question, etc.)
   b) State the evidence rule number if you know it (404, 608, etc.).
   c) A combination of the above
      ("Objection, Improper Impeachment, R613")
4) Stop talking and listen to the judge.
   Be prepared to state reasons for your objection and to make an argument to support your position.

How to Respond to an Objection
1) Speak to the judge, not the lawyer who objected.
2) Explain to the judge why your evidence should be admissible. ("Your Honor, that statement is not hearsay because I am not offering it for the truth, but rather to show notice.")
3) If you recognize that you did not lay an appropriate foundation for the evidence, explain that you will do that. ("Your Honor, I will lay the foundation.")
4) If you recognize that the opposing counsel was objecting to the form of your question, which most often happens on your direct examination, simply say, "I'll rephrase." Rephrase the question and move on with your witness examination. Do not get sidetracked by the opposing counsel who might have objected just to throw you off track.
5) For any physical piece of evidence, statement, or testimony that you will be introducing, prepare in advance and have a reason why you believe that evidence is admissible. Be ready to make that argument to the judge.
6) If the objection is to relevance, and you think you will be able to show that it is relevant after additional testimony, say to the judge, "I will connect it up in a few questions Your Honor." Such a statement is equivalent of saying "trust me." If you do say that, you had better connect it up later or the judge will not trust you in the future.

If You are a Judge Who Has to Rule on the Objection
1) If the specific objection was not identified, turn to the lawyer who made the objection and say, "Basis?" - Meaning, "What is the legal basis for your objection?"
2) After the lawyer has put their specific objection on the record, turn to the proponent (the lawyer who is attempting to introduce the evidence), and say, "What is your response?"
3) Allow more argument if necessary. "Counsel, how do you respond to that argument?"
4) After the arguments are completed, make your ruling.
   A) "Sustained" - meaning you agree with the objection, and you will exclude the evidence.
   B) "Overruled" - meaning you agree with the proponent of the evidence, and the evidence will be admissible.
   C) Reserve your ruling until the end of the trial. ("I will reserve my decision on this issue until the close of the testimony.")
   D) Ask lawyers to submit a written memorandum on the issue when the trial ends so you have a better understanding of the issue.

Multiple Lawyers and Multiple Clients
If two or more lawyers represent one client, only one of the lawyers can object to each of the witnesses. Only one lawyer can make objections for each witness, e.g. if you do the direct, you are the only one who can object on cross. They cannot "tag team" and both object or respond to objections for single witness. If there are multiple parties who each have their own lawyer, each lawyer must make their own objection to have the objections preserved for appeal.

Judges Apply the Rules of Evidence More Loosely in Nonjury Trials.
Many jurisdictions apply a presumption that a trial judge will ignore inadmissible evidence. I doubt that is true. What is to the questionable evidence is very seldom basis for reversing a verdict in a nonjury trial.

The Key to Objection is Rule 103
There is a rhyme to this phrase. "Key" rhymes with "103." Rule 103 holds the key to understanding the process of objections. Read that rule very carefully. The full rule follows.

Important Points about Rule 103 include:
1) The objection must be timely and state the specific ground for the objection, unless it is apparent from the context.
2) If the evidence was admitted, appellate courts do not have to consider the issue unless a specific ground for the objection was timely stated.
3) If the evidence was excluded, the appellate court needs information about what the excluded evidence was going to be. That information must be provided by an "offer of proof" unless the information was apparent from the context.
4) The judge can make statements for the record about the objection, the evidence, the form of the evidence, the ruling, and can require an offer of proof in question and answer form.
5) An error is not sufficient to reverse the trial unless a "substantial right" of a party is affected.
6) Even if there was no objection at trial, "plain errors" affecting "substantial rights" can result in a reversal on appeal.

Pa.R.E. 103. Rulings on Evidence

(a) **Preserving a Claim of Error.** A party may claim error in a ruling to admit or exclude evidence only:
> (1) if the ruling admits evidence, a party, on the record:
>> (A) makes a timely objection, motion to strike, or motion *in limine*; and
>> B) states the specific ground, unless it was apparent from the context; or
>
> (2) if the ruling excludes evidence, a party informs the court of its substance by an offer of proof, unless the substance was apparent from the context.

(b) **Not Needing to Renew an Objection or Offer of Proof.** Once the court rules definitively on the record--either before or at trial--a party need not renew an objection or offer of proof to preserve a claim of error for appeal.

(c) **Court's Statement About the Ruling; Directing an Offer of Proof.** The court may make any statement about the character or form of the evidence, the objection made, and the ruling. The court may direct that an offer of proof be made in question-and-answer form.

(d) **Preventing the Jury from Hearing Inadmissible Evidence.** To the extent practicable, the court must conduct a jury trial so that inadmissible evidence is not suggested to the jury by any means.

The Most Common Substantive Objections Are Based on The Rules of Evidence and Constitutional Issues. Each article within the evidence code has one or more common types of objections, such as:

General provisions	100s
Objections	
Preliminary questions	
Limited admissibility	
Remainder of or related writings	
Judicial notice	200s
Presumptions	300s
Relevance	400s
Privileges	500s
Witnesses	600s
Competence	
Impeachment	
Opinions and expert testimony	700s
Hearsay	800s
Authentication	900s
Best evidence (original writings)	1000s

Motions in Limine

In a jury trial, lawyers often make a pretrial motion in limine, which is a motion to exclude or admit certain evidence. In jury trials, the motion is made outside the presence of the jury. The judge's ruling on the motion in limine can 1) prevent inadmissible evidence from being heard by a jury, or 2) allow lawyers to know that they can go forward and attempt to introduce certain evidence without risking a mistrial. Motions in limine are probably not necessary in a nonjury trial because the judge will have to hear the potentially inadmissible evidence before ruling on the motion. Therefore, even if the evidence would be ruled inadmissible, the trial judge who will be the trier of fact will have already heard the inadmissible evidence. Judges in nonjury trials are presumed to ignore inadmissible evidence.

Phrases and Questions that Suggest Inadmissible or Objectionable Information is Coming.

Lawyer: "<u>In summary,</u> witness you've testified that…"
Likely objection: Asked and answered

Lawyer: "Witness, <u>what if I told you that another witness testified</u> that…"
Likely objection: Calls for speculation, argumentative, etc.

Inadequate Objections – Not Specific Enough
"I object."
"Objection to the form of the question."
"Insufficient foundation."
"Inadmissible."
"Incompetent, irrelevant, and immaterial."

Offers of Proof are:
1) sometimes just summary statements by a lawyer of what the evidence would be if the lawyer were given an opportunity to call the witness or introduce the exhibit. ("Your Honor, if the witness would be allowed to testify, she would say that ……"), and,
2) sometimes offers of proof are questions of the lawyer and answers of the witness given in question and answer form outside the presence of the jury. (Q1 A1; Q2 A2; Q3 A3)

The Impact of Objections in Nonjury Trials – Seldom Reversed
Many objections, especially to the forms of questions, seldom result in reversals even in jury trials. And it would be extremely rare for an appellate court to reverse a nonjury trial decision based on an objection to the form of a question or the form of an answer. Although objection battles on the forms of questions do take place in jury trials, such battles are less important in nonjury trials because the judge is presumed to ignore inadmissible evidence and decide the case only on evidence that was admissible.

Common Phrases from Court Opinions Summarizing That Inadmissible Evidence in A Nonjury Trial Will Not Result in A Reversal Include:
- "Trial judges often have access to inadmissible and highly prejudicial information and are presumed to be able to discount or disregard it."
- "In bench trials, judges routinely hear inadmissible evidence that they are presumed to ignore."
- "The presumption that the trial judge disregarded all inadmissible evidence in reaching his decision."
- "It is presumed that improper evidence taken under objection was given no weight in reaching the final conclusion [in a nonjury trial] unless the contrary appears."
- "A judge, as factfinder, is presumed to disregard inadmissible evidence and consider only competent evidence."
- "A judge "must be presumed to be able to disregard inflammatory evidence"

Common Objections to the Form of the Question

Objections to the form of the question often have no clear answers or standards. Many judges and lawyers might disagree as to whether some question is improper or not. If a rule is cited when making the objection, it would usually be Rule 611.

Argumentative (also called **Harassing, Badgering**) **(R611)**
An argumentative question asks the witness to accept the examiner's summary, inference, or conclusion rather than a fact. Often the objector is trying to protect a witness during cross-examination.
Examples of Argumentative Questions:
"Isn't what you told this judge on its face ridiculous?"
"How can you expect the judge to believe that?"
"Are you telling this court that you don't know what a machete is?"
"Do you really expect the judge to believe that?"
"Do you mean to tell me...?"
"Doesn't it seem strange that...?"
"Your kind of the hatchet man down here for the D.A.s Office, aren't you?"
"It wouldn't bother you any, to come in here and lie from the time you started to the time you stopped, would it?"

Asked and Answered: This rule is violated by repeating the same question, asked by the same lawyer, to get the same answer, from the same witness, and is not permitted under R611. A question which has previously been asked and answered is being asked again. The rule prevents cumulative testimony R403. Repeating the testimony of a witness who has previously given the same testimony after being asked the same question by the same lawyer in not permitted. However, similar questions are often permitted if the identical information is not repeated. This objection does not apply to prevent the same questions being asked on cross-examination that were asked on direct examination. It does not prevent asking identical questions of different witnesses, nor does it prevent a lawyer representing a co-party from asking the same questions to the same witness again.

Assuming Facts Not in Evidence. This rule is violated when part of a question (usually the first part) assumes the truth of a fact that is in dispute but has not yet been proved at trial. Such a question is unfair because it cannot be answered without conceding the unproven fact. Assuming facts not in evidence may be an attempt to bring into the trial information that the lawyer is not able to prove by other means. However, questions that assume facts are permitted on cross-examination to impeach a witness's credibility.

Examples of assuming facts not in evidence:
"When did you stop beating your wife?" (assumes previous beatings)
"Did you know their business dropped 50% because of what the defendant did?" (assumes the defendant did the same thing)
"How long after you purchased the items were they given to the defendant?" (assumes the purchase)

Responses:
"I will connect it up later."(Which just means, "Judge trust me and allow a few more questions." And, if you request permission to "connect up later" you'd better be able to connect it up or the judge will no longer trust you.)
"I have a good faith basis for assuming those facts. I would like to proceed without further tipping my hand."
"This is criminal case and the defendant has a Sixth Amendment right to fully cross-examine the witness."

Beyond the Scope (of a prior examination). Questions on redirect examination cannot go into subject matters that have not been covered in the previous cross-examination. Similarly, questions on re-cross examination cannot go beyond the scope of redirect examination. Redirect examination is limited to issues raised by the opposing lawyer on cross-examination. If the questions go beyond the issues raised on cross, the objection will be valid.

Responses.
"Your Honor, I'm allowed to go into this area because it goes to the witness's credibility."

Note well: Cross-examination is not limited to the subjects covered on direct examination. If it was so limited, the cross examiner would be prohibited from fully examining the witness and exposing weaknesses in the direct exam. If a "beyond the scope" objection is raised to a cross-examination question, the best response probably would be, "Your Honor, R611 allows me to cross on the subject matter of direct examination and "matters affecting the witness's credibility." My cross goes to credibility."

Compound Question.
A compound question has two or more separate questions in a single question, and usually contains the words "and" or "or." A simple "yes" or "no" answer to the question will be unclear. If the witness asked answers "yes" or "no," it is not clear if the "yes" or "no" applies to all the multiple parts of the question or just one part.
Examples:
> "On that day, you went shopping <u>and</u> to the beach, didn't you?"
> "Did you determine the time of death by interviewing witnesses <u>and</u> by requesting the autopsy report?"
> "On that Saturday, did you send the email <u>and</u> also call the banker?"

Cumulative (R403)
Cumulative questions ask for the same information from the same witness multiple times (like asked and answered) or ask multiple witnesses to establish the same facts.

Lack of Foundation (R901)
A lack of foundation objection arises when the lawyer asks a question before establishing the preliminary facts which would permit the questions. The evidence lacks testimony as to its authenticity or source.

Leading Question (R611)

A leading question improperly suggests the answer that the lawyer wants on direct examination. Another test is that the question contains the desired answer. The danger is that the question will make the witness agree with a false suggestion. Often leading questions start with phrases like - "Isn't it true that…" "Did…?" Or ends with "…,right?" Questions that start with the word "So" should be at least a yellow flag that the question might be leading. Although some questions are obviously leading, lawyers and judges often have very different interpretations of what a leading question is. Be prepared to quickly rephrase your question if an objection to it is sustained. Whether or not a question that contains the phrase "whether or not" is leading has been subject to much debate. A lawyer's nonverbal behavior or voice inflection is sometimes considered when determining whether a question is leading.

Leading questions are permissible for preliminary matters, when a party calls a hostile witness or an adverse witness (Rule 611) or when a witness is very young, very old, or mentally challenged. Leading questions are also common and proper on direct examination when laying foundations because under Rule 104 the rules of evidence do not apply, except for privileges, when asking preliminary questions about the admissibility of evidence. Leading questions are also permissible when they are used like a topic sentence in a paragraph to move a witness on direct examination to another part of the scene. For example," Did there come a time when you went into the store?" Of course, the lawyer could get the same result by simply making the statement, "Now I want to ask you some questions about what you did when you went into the store." It is a common belief that the more a lawyer leads on direct examination, the less credibility the witness will have because the witness looks like they are being told what to say during the examination.

Motion to strike

Motions to strike are used two ways. First, Rule of Civil Procedure 12(f) allows for motions to strike certain pleadings. Second, Motions to strike, under evidence R103, are treated similarly to objections and ask the judge to strike inadmissible testimony from the record if the witness has just said the objectionable words. Of course, "striking" is not really striking. The inadmissible words are not removed from the court records but remain in the record even if the testimony is "stricken." The opposing lawyer can ask the judge to instruct the jury to disregard the "stricken" testimony, but psychologically, such an instruction to "disregard" the testimony might highlight the testimony for the jury. Tough choices to make.

Narrative Question, or Calls for A Narrative Answer, or simply Narrative Answer

A narrative objection can refer to a question that asks a witness to tell a story rather than to state only a few specific facts, or refer to witness' answer which is several sentences, or even paragraphs, long. On one hand, narrative answers allow the witness to easily include inadmissible evidence, but on the other hand, a narrative story might more likely provide truthful facts.

Examples of narrative questions:
"What did you do that day?"
"Tell us about the accident."
"Now tell us what everyone said and did at that point."
"What happened that night?"
"How did the accident happen?"
Ans: "First thing I got up and I… Then I went to… After that I … She told me that… And I immediately saw the …"

Non-Responsive Answer: The non-responsive answer objection is made to an answer that does not answer the question that was asked. Simply, the witness does not answer the question asked by the lawyer. The witness is trying to make their own point and take control of the testimony. A problem with nonresponsive answers is that the witness is volunteering information that might be irrelevant or unfairly prejudicial. <u>In theory, only the lawyer asking the question can object to a non-responsive answer</u>. Some judges will only allow this objection from the lawyer who is asking the question. If the objection is sustained, it is often followed by a motion to strike the answer from the record. If the opposing lawyer is considering making a non-responsive answer objection, they are should consider some other appropriate objection such as "irrelevant," "unfairly prejudicial," or "lack of foundation."

Example of a non-responsive answers:
Q: "Did you see the other driver get out of his car right after the accident?"
A: "He told me he had insurance."

Q: "Weren't you the last person the victim saw on the night of his death?"
A: "I had nothing to do with that!"

Speculation – Calls for Speculation – Lack Person Knowledge. (R602)

A speculation objection is proper if the lawyer asks the witness a question that the witness has no personal knowledge about, or the witness testifies about something they have not perceived. A red flag signaling a call for speculation is often a question that starts with, Isn't it possible that…?" A better phrasing to accomplish the same objective would be to focus the question on the witness's personal knowledge and experience by asking for the same information but stating it as follows, "You don't know whether or not…, do you?"

Examples of a question calling for speculation:
"What do you think he was thinking about at that time?"
"Why would she do something like that?"

Vague and Ambiguous Question: Vague and ambiguous questions are asked in ways that are incomprehensible, incomplete, or the answer will be ambiguous. If you, as the opposing lawyer, do not understand the question asked by your opponent, then the witness probably does not understand the question either. Object.

Other Objections

Golden Rule

The Golden Rule objection is made when the opposing counsel places the trier of fact (judge or jury) in the same situation that the case is about.

Examples of a Golden Rule objection:
"Your Honor, what would you have done in a situation like that?"
"Ladies and gentlemen of the jury, would you want someone like that coming into your neighborhood?"

Speaking Objections
A speaking objection is a lawyer's attempt to influence the jury by speaking to the jury by using the objection. Although such objections are very disfavored by judges in jury trials, in nonjury trials such objections can be used to make an argument to the trial judge and influence the decision to be made on the objection.

Examples of speaking objections:
>"Well Judge, I am going to strongly object to this procedure. I feel that I am being sandbagged here and I don't appreciate it."
>
>"Your honor, it doesn't matter what the answer is. Opposing counsel just wants to make a statement. He doesn't care what this witness says,"

Coaching the witness
Such objections can be used to communicate with and coach a witness.

Example of coaching the witness through an objection:
>"Objection. The witness couldn't possibly know that answer."
>   Witness then responds by saying, "I don't know."

Relevance
Questions in a case about some other person, some other event, and some other time, are irrelevant unless the judge find such questions to be relevant in this particular case for a special reason such as to show bias or relevant in this case under Rule 404(b). I call such irrelevant evidence <u>P.E.T. evidence</u> and tell my students that PET evidence is not admissible - evidence about some other <u>Person, or Event, or Time</u>. Furthermore, questions about "**what most people do**" are almost always irrelevant.

Examples of irrelevant "what most people do" objections:
>"<u>Don't most people </u>know that…?"
>"Don't most people speed when their car is headed downhill?"

A Few Useful Definitions

Stipulation: Agreement between opposing lawyers to admit certain evidence without the normal in-court proof. The trier of fact then assumes the fact to have been proven.

Offer of Proof:
A statement by a lawyer describing E that the lawyer wants admitted. Proponent summarizes the substance of the excluded evidence to the judge to persuade the judge and to make a record for appeal. – R103

Motion in Limine:
A pre-trial motion seeking a ruling to admit or exclude evidence.

Limited Admissibility:
Evidence can be admitted for one purpose or against one party, but not admitted for another purpose or against another party. – R105

Intrinsic Impeachment - out of the witness' own mouth (almost always) on cross-examination. After a direct exam, the witness is impeached on cross. Almost always permissible.

Extrinsic Impeachment – impeachment coming for the testimony of another witness or the use of a document to impeach. If a witness is not impeached on cross by the opponent's questions, not all types of impeachment are permitted as extrinsic impeachment. The most common limitation is R608(b) – prior bad acts related to dishonestly.

Collateral - relevant only to discredit; does not go to a material matter.

A List of Common Possible Objections

Ambiguous	Improper opinion
Argumentative	Improper rehabilitation
Asked and answered	Inadmissible opinion
Assumes facts not in evidence	Incompetent witness
Authentication	Incomplete Inflammatory
Badgering	Insufficient foundation
Best evidence	Irrelevant (Relevance)
Beyond the scope	Lack of foundation
Bias	Lack of personal knowledge
Bolstering	Leading question
Calls for a conclusion	Misleading
Calls for speculation	Misquotes a witness or exhibit
Chain of custody	Misquotes evidence
Collateral	Misstates witness
Competence	More prejudicial than probative
Compound question	Motion to strike
Compromise / Settlement offer	Narrative
Confrontation (lack of)	(Question calls for a narrative)
Confusing	Narrative answer
Counsel is testifying	Non-responsive
Cumulative	Nothing pending
Document speaks for itself	Outside the scope of cross
Expert (Improper opinion)	Overly broad or general
Expert (not qualified)	Parole evidence rule
Habit	Personal knowledge
Harassing the witness	Prejudice (unfair)
Hearsay	Privilege communication
Hypothetical question misused	Relevance
Improper character evidence	Speculation/ Opinion/ Lack of
Improper characterization	personal knowledge
Improper impeachment	Unintelligible
	Vague

There are many more possible objections, limited only by the lawyer's imagination.

Judges and the local legal culture in your jurisdiction may have other rules or approaches to objections that are not touched on in this handbook. Ask around and learn about them.

Evidentiary Foundations

Foundations - Predicates - Laying the Foundation

Foundations are questions asked by a lawyer to set the groundwork (the foundation) for admitting evidence at trial. The asking of these questions is often referred to as "**laying the foundation**" for the evidence. The word "**predicates,**" when used by trial lawyers, refers to a series of form or sample questions that a lawyer must ask to establish the facts, events, or conditions which are required by the rules of evidence or caselaw before presenting other evidence. Predicates are the questions that are asked when laying the foundation for other evidence. The evidentiary foundation is like the foundation for a building. It provides a solid basis for building up the structure of the case at trial. The necessary foundational questions are not always obvious by reading the rules of evidence.

Foundations may come from local legal culture ("That's the way we do things in this jurisdiction") or from a lawyer or judges prior experience ("That's the way I was taught to do it," or ("That's what I think works best,"), so that's what I am requiring you to do."

Evidentiary Foundations A-17
Foundations – Laying the Foundation - Predicates A-17
Evidentiary Foundations Index A-18
Bare-Bones Foundations A-20
Admissibility v. Weight A-21
Example of Admissibility and Weight A-21
3 Simple Questions A-22
Steps for Introducing Exhibits A-23
The Common Evidentiary Foundations A-25
The Phrases to Move Evidence into a Trial A-26
Useful Points to Remember A-27
    Into Evidence A-27
    Make an Offer of Proof A-27
    Hearsay Within Hearsay A-27
    Public Records Do Not Have to Be Open to The Public A-27
    Compute Generated Record Is Not Hearsay A-27
    Emails Offered to Show Notice, Knowledge or Fear Are Not Hearsay .. A-27
    Demonstrative Evidence A-27
    Chain of Custody A-27
    Distinctive Characteristics A-27
    Authenticate with Personal Knowledge and Distinctive Characteristics . A-28
    Affidavits Are Hearsay and Inadmissible at Trial A-28
    Harrowing A-28
    OTP – Offered to Prove A-28
    Rules Do Not Explain How to Introduce Evidence in Court A-28
    Laying A Foundation Is Like A Sport A-28
    Mark, Show, Approach, Foundational Questions, Offer A-28
    Magic Words A-29
    Speak in Generic Terms A-29
    Publish Means to Show Them Now A-29
    Chain of Custody Is Only for Fungible Items or Samples to Test ... A-29
    Basic Tasks A Trial Lawyer Should Be Able to Do A-29
    Best Evidentiary Foundation Resources A-29
    Important Evidence Rules to Guide You - 103, 104, 901, 612, 613,
        801, 803(6), 901, 902(11), 902(13&14), 105, 106, 1006 .... A-30
    Opponent Has the Burden on The Issue of Trustworthiness A-31
Basic Foundation & Impeachment Examples A-32
    Nita Liquor Commission Facts A-33
    Officer Bier's Report A-34
    Diagram of Cut-Rate Liquor Store Area A-35
    Photograph of A Scene A-36
    Diagram of The Scene A-37
    Real Evidence – Thunderbird Wine Bottle A-38
    Offering A Contract into Evidence A-39

Refreshing Memory – Anything A-40
Writing Used to Refresh Memory – R612 .... A-42
Refreshing Memory with A Leading Question A-43
Recorded Recollection (Author's Rule) A-44
Business Records - Custodian of Records – R803(6) A-46
Business Records Are KRAP A-47
Self-Authenticating Business Records Form - Texas A-48
Demonstrative Evidence - Similar to The Real Item A-49
Impeachment - Prior Written Inconsistent Statement A-50
Impeachment by Omission A-52
Impeachment by Inconsistent Oral Deposition A-54
Impeachment - Inconsistent Oral Deposition - Short Form A-55
Impeachment - Inconsistent Oral Deposition - Long Form A-56
Impeachment - Inconsistent Oral Statement A-57
Learned Treatises Use on Direct Exam - R803(18) A-58
3 Key Points for Using Learned Treatises A-59
Learned Treatises: Use on Cross - R803(18) A-60
Voicemail and Phone Conversations A-61
Digital Evidence – Electronically Stored Information – ESI A-63
A Variety of Different Standards A-63
Distinctive Characteristics and Circumstantial Evidence A-65
Presenting Digital Evidence from A Cell Phone in Court A-66
Digital Evidence and Self-Authentication A-67
Digital Evidence Foundations A-63
Email – Outgoing A-68
Email – Incoming A-69
Text Message – Received by Witness A-70
Social Media: Facebook, Instagram, Snapchat, Twitter A-71
Internet Website – Web Posting A-72
Fax – Incoming A-73
Foundation for Expert Opinion A-74
History and Restyling of The Federal Rules of Evidence A-78
Teaching Evidence since 4 B.C. A-79
Other Evidence Books in This Series by John Barkai A-80
Dedication A-82
About the Author A-82

Bare-Bones Foundations

The foundations provided in this handbook are designed to be brief, what I call "bare-bones foundations." A "bare-bones" foundation uses the minimum necessary questions to admit a piece of evidence or testimony and is less concerned about the "weight" of the evidence to be admitted. Bare-bones foundations are commonly used in non-jury trials. The judge, as trier of fact, should understand the elements of each foundation. On the other hand, what I call **"advocacy foundations"** are more common in jury trials where a jury of laypeople will make the important factual determinations in the case. An advocacy foundation uses much more than the bare minimum number of questions to lay the foundation, with additional questions going to enhance the persuasiveness of the sponsoring witness and the evidence. For example, when using a police officer's report to refresh memory, for recorded recollection, or to impeach, the additional questions might include questions relating to the training or conduct of the officer, such as:

"Did you have training in writing reports?"

"How much training?"

"When you are writing your report, you know that your supervisor will read some of your reports?"

"You know that your future assignments might depend on the quality of your written reports?"

"Do you normally reread your report before submitting it?"

"Do you check your report for accuracy before submitting it?"

Admissibility v. Weight

Foundations are sometimes necessary for evidence to be admissible. As such, they go to the issue of "admissibility," which is about "can" the evidence be included in the trial so that the trier of fact (judge or jury) can consider that evidence in decision-making. On the other hand, the "weight" of evidence is the "value" to be given to the piece of evidence by the trier of fact. Trial judgments are usually determined by which party's admitted evidence is more persuasive, and has the party met the burden of persuasion to the necessary standard (such as: "preponderance of the evidence" or "beyond a reasonable doubt").

Example of Admissibility and Weight

Assume the trial is about a fight. One person says, "He hit me." The other person says, "I did not." Both statements will be admissible, but the trier of fact, after listening to other facts and witnesses, will probably assign different weights or values to the testimony of the two people. Typically, one person will be considered more credible or believable than the other person. The more reliable person's testimony it is said to be given greater weight. It is that weight of the evidence that will eventually lead to a decision for one party or the other. A common statement made by a judge when an opposing party argues against the admissibility of testimony or other evidence is, "That goes to weight, not admissibility." Such a statement by a judge means, "You just lost your battle to exclude that evidence from the trial, but you can still argue that your case is stronger and more persuasive than your opponent's case is."

3 Simple Questions

After handing a physical item to a witness and saying for the record, "Let me show you what has been marked as proposed exhibit number one," the foundation for some physical pieces of evidence can be established with as few as three questions:

> 1) Q: What is it?
>
> 2) Q: How do you know that?
>
> 3) Q: Is it in the same condition as it was on the day of …?"
> (Or, "Is that a fair and accurate representation of the item as it was on …?").

Steps for Introducing Exhibits

> **Preliminary steps are:**
> 1) **Have the exhibit marked for identification**
> 2) **Show the proposed exhibit to opposing counsel**
> 3) **Ask permission to approach the witness with the proposed exhibit**

1. **History - How the witness knows the exhibit.**
   Offer some testimony that the witness <u>knows</u> or is <u>familiar with</u> the evidence – such as a document, physical item, photo, diagram, scene, text message, email - or recalls the statement. Even if the witness has only seen the exhibit once before or has just been to the scene shown in the photograph once before, <u>once is enough</u>.

2. **The Litany (a ritualistic repetition of foundational questions)**
   a) Ask the court clerk to **mark the item** (using numbers or letters). The clerk will decide which system to use. In more serious cases in the jurisdiction's higher courts (typically where jury trials are allowed), exhibits are usually required to be marked at least before trial starts, and often during pretrial conferences.
   b) **Show opposing counsel** (this will prevent interruptions) and say, "Let the record reflect that I am showing the defense what has been marked as plaintiff's proposed exhibit number one."
   c) Ask the judge for **permission to approach** the witness. "May I approach the witness?"
   - **Q: "I show you what has been marked as** Plaintiff's (Prosecution's) (Defense's) proposed exhibit # x (or exhibit #x for identification purposes) **and ask whether you can identify it"** (You expect a "yes" answer here.)
   - **Q: "What is it?"** (They describe it in general terms. "It is the contract/photo of the scene/weapon recovered/drugs seized/diagram of the area/etc.")
   - **Q: "How do you know that?"** (They answer – "I recognize it. It has my signature on it. / I have been there many times before. / I put my initials on it and the defendant's name/etc.")

3. Show Condition or Comparison or Accuracy

Some comparison must be made between the exhibit in court and when the witness became familiar with the exhibit out-of-court. Of the examples that follow, only one such question is necessary.

- "Is this in the **same** condition as when you... [first saw it...seized it...etc.]?"
- "Is this in the **same or substantially** the same condition.... as when you..."   (for item or document)
- "Is it a **fair and accurate representation of** the ... **as it was that day**?"   (for diagram or pictures)
- "**Has it changed** in any significant way?"
- "**How does it compare** to the item you saw that day?"

4. Move or Offer the Exhibit into Evidence

"Your honor, **I offer the exhibit into evidence**." - or, "I move the exhibit into evidence."

You could instead say, "I offer proposed exhibit # 1 into evidence as exhibit # 1," but why make it so confusing? Just say, "I offer the exhibit into evidence."

The judge <u>might</u> ask the opposing counsel, "Any objections?" but the opponent should object immediately after the proponent offers the exhibit, if there is an objection to the admissibility (not the weight). The judge should allow "voir dire" (immediate cross examination limited to the foundation and the admissibility) by the opponent of the exhibit.

The Common Evidentiary Foundations

Physical Items
Photograph (printed)
Diagram of scene
Physical item seized at scene

Common Documents
Refreshing memory
Recorded recollection
Business records in paper
Business records – and self-authentication under R902
Deposition Impeachment (see below)

Records and Treatises
Public record
Learned treatise –
    Use on direct supporting your expert
    Use on cross attacking their expert

Digital Evidence – from the internet, a cell phone, or a computer
    Also called - ESI – Electronically Stored Information
Emails
Text message – issues of incompleteness
Social Media - Facebook, Instagram, Twitter, Snapchat
Website posting
Voicemail recording
Videos, including on cell phone
Photo on cell phone
Fax
Chatroom conversations

Impeachment
    Impeaching by Prior Written Inconsistent statement
    Impeaching by Omission in Prior Written Statement
    Impeaching by Prior Oral Inconsistent statement
    Impeaching by Inconsistent Oral Deposition Transcript

Phrases to Move Evidence into a Trial

(Pick one and always use it)

"I offer the exhibit into evidence." (By far the easiest to use)

"Your Honor, I ask that what's been previously marked as Plaintiff's Exhibit A for Identification be admitted into evidence as Plaintiff's A."

"At this time, we offer Plaintiff's A for identification into evidence as Plaintiff's exhibit A."

"The Government at this time, would move to introduce Government's Exhibit No. 2 into evidence."

"Your Honor, we'd offer Defense Exhibit B into evidence."

"Your Honor, I move that Plaintiff's Exhibit 3 be introduced into evidence."

"We offer Exhibit A into evidence."

"Your honor, I would like to submit People's exhibit 'A' into evidence."

"We would ask the Court to admit State's Exhibit 4 for Identification as State's 4."

Useful Points to Remember

Offering something "into evidence" means that in a jury trial the exhibit can go into the jury room and be reviewed as many times as the jurors want to look at it.

Make an Offer of Proof – if your evidence is not admitted. R103.

Hearsay within hearsay – statements incorporated into other statements need an additional hearsay exception to be admissible. R805 Hearsay Within Hearsay.

Public records do not have to be "open to the public" but rather are reports and records created by public (government) employees. R803(8)

A record automatically generated by a computer - is not hearsay (computer generated records). No assertion by a person.

Email offered to show notice, knowledge, or fear are not assertions and therefore not hearsay. In a contract or consent form, the words have independent legal significance, which means they operate to form a contract even if they are not true.

Demonstrative evidence – demonstrates or represents some real evidence. Also sometimes called **illustrative evidence**, as compared to **real evidence**, which as some historical connection to the case - such as being the drugs, the gun, etc.

A **"chain of custody" is required for fungible items** that cannot be identified and distinguished on sight, such as drugs, alcohol, and blood examples - indistinguishable as grains of sand. Often, they are taken into custody and forwarded for laboratory testing. The "chain" makes sure the evidence that is tested is connected to the correct case.

Distinctive characteristics Evidence tags with initials and case names make items unique and should qualify as a **"Distinctive characteristic"** under R901(b)(4) for authentication purposes.

The most common method to introduce physical and documentary evidence is **using personal knowledge and distinctive characteristics.** R901(b)(1)&(4)

Affidavits are hearsay and not admissible at trial. However, affidavits can be used in summary judgment proceedings if the statements in the affidavits would be admissible in court if testified to by the declarant with personal knowledge. Therefore, lawyers should not be signing affidavits for summary judgement. Potential witnesses with personal knowledge of the facts must sign the affidavits.

HARROWing - a Barkai mnemonic/acronym formed from the first letters of evidence concepts most likely to impact admissibility decisions. Always think of HARROWing when a physical item is going to be introduced, especially if the item is a document or a physical item with words on it. **H**earsay R800s, **A**uthentication R900s, **R**elevance R401, **R**elevance R403, **O**riginal **W**ritings (Best Evidence) R1000s. HARROWing applies to ESI (Electronically Stored Information) such as emails, texts, websites, etc.

OTP - what is the evidence "Offered to Prove?" OTP impacts relevance, admissibility, and the necessary foundation.

The rules of evidence do not tell you how to introduce exhibits although some rules do list the foundational elements which must be included in foundational questions. The hearsay exceptions of Recorded Recollection R803(5) and Records of a Regular Conducted Activity (business records) R803(6) are examples of hearsay exceptions that are so complicated that a novice trial lawyer might want to have the rule in front of them when attempting to lay the foundation.

Laying a foundation is like a sport. Practice before the game.

Steps: Mark/Pre-Mark, Show, Approach, Foundational Questions, Offer
  Mark exhibits: 1 day before trial or prior to trial – depending on the court rules.

Magic Words: "**in the same or substantially the same condition**" or "**fair and accurate representation**," or "**fairly accurate representation**," or "**fairly represent**."

Speak in generic terms when talking about exhibits until the witness identifies the exhibit: "Proposed exhibit # 1" or "Exhibit # 1 for identification purposes," not "Your report," or "Photo of the scene."

To "publish" an exhibit means to show the exhibit to the jury or ask the judge to look at the exhibit now.

Chain of evidence is usually only necessary for fungible items (identical - they all look the same), or items that need testing – drugs, alcohol, blood, DNA. Not every "kink in the link" of the chain of evidence makes evidence inadmissible. Authentication only requires production of evidence "sufficient to support a finding," R901(a)(1), which is a low standard.

Basic tasks that every trial lawyer should be able to do
- introduce documents, physical items, photographs
- refresh memory (almost always done on direct)
- use the recollection recorded hearsay exception (almost always done on direct).
- impeach (almost always done on cross); inconsistent statements & omissions.

The Best Foundation Resources
- Grimm, Joseph & Capra, Best Practices for Authenticating Digital Evidence 69 Baylor L.R. 1 (2017)
- Evidentiary Foundations for Government Attorneys (2015) (from National Attorneys General Training & Research Institute) - (JB: It contains many simple foundations.)
- Edward Imwinkelried, Evidentiary Foundations, (10th ed. 2018) – (The classic source for foundations, but less than you might want about ESI foundations, and more than you might want in the middle of trial.)
- Deanne Siemer, Laying Foundations and Meeting Objections (4th ed. 2013)

Laying Foundations

Important Evidence Rules to Guide You

Pa.R.E. 103. Ruling on Evidence – (Re: Offer of Proof) – explains how to protect your record if your evidence is excluded.

Pa.R.E. 104 Preliminary questions.
   (a) **In General.** The court must decide any preliminary question about whether a witness is qualified, a privilege exists, or evidence is admissible. In so deciding, the court is not bound by evidence rules, except those on privilege.
   [**JB**: meaning you can lead on direct for foundations.]
   (b) **Relevance that Depends on a Fact.** When the relevance of evidence depends on whether a fact exists, proof must be introduced sufficient to support a finding that the fact does exist...
[**JB**: that is a low threshold.]

Pa.R.E. 901 Authenticating or Identifying Evidence.
(a) **In General.** Unless stipulated, to satisfy the requirement of authenticating or identifying an item of evidence, the proponent must produce evidence sufficient to support a finding that the item is what the proponent claims it is. [**JB**: that is a low threshold]
(b) **Examples.** The following are examples only ...
   (1) **Testimony of a Witness with Knowledge.** Testimony that an item is what it is claimed to be.
   (4) **Distinctive Characteristics and the Like.** The appearance, contents, substance, internal patterns, or other distinctive characteristics of the item, taken together with all the circumstances.
   (7) **Evidence About Public Records.**
   (9) **Evidence About a Process or System.**

R612 Writing Used to Refresh a Witness's Memory. Witness does not need to be the author. Anything can be used to refresh memory - even "my left shoe" – My in-class example.

R613 Witness's Prior Statement. Impeachment by inconsistent statements and omissions.

R801(d)(1) Not Hearsay: A Declarant-Witness's Prior Statement. (Inconsistent under oath, consistent, or prior ID)

R803(6) Records of a Regularly Conducted Activity
(**JB**: business records are **KRAP**)
   (**K**ept in the course, **R**egular practice, **A**t or near the time, **P**ersonal knowledge)

R902 Evidence That Is Self-Authenticating

Pa.R.E. 902(11) Certified Domestic Records of a Regularly Conducted Activity. [Note: There are many certification forms available on the internet.]

Pa.R.E. 902(13) Certified Records Generated by an Electronic Process or System.
[Note: **Pennsylvania has adopted** this rule.]

Pa.R.E. 902(14) Certified Data Copied from an Electronic Device, Storage Medium, or File.
[Note: **Pennsylvania has adopted** this rule.]

Pa.R.E. 105 Limiting Evidence That is Not Admissible
Limited Admissibility (admitted against only one party or for a limited purpose)

Pa.R.E. 106 Remainder of or Related Writings or Recorded Statements - Remainder of / related writing [JB: admit now]

Pa.R.E. 1006 Summaries... voluminous writings which cannot conveniently be examined in court.

The Opponent Has the Burden
On the Issue of Trustworthiness of Records

Burden of showing a record lacks trustworthiness is on the opponent in the Federal rules - R803(6)(7)(8) ... "and, the opponent does not show ...a lack of trustworthiness."

Note: **Pennsylvania has adopted** these burden rules in Pa.R.E. 803(6) and 8903(8), although it did not adopt rule 803(7).

Basic Foundations & Impeachment Examples

Several of the following foundation and impeachment examples are based upon the facts of

Nita Liquor Commission v. Cut-Rate Liquor and Jones*

In this famous, fictional case from NITA (National Institute of Trial Advocacy), Walter Watkins was observed going into the Cut-Rate Liquor Store by Officer Bier and his partner from their unmarked car which was parked across the street from the liquor store. The officers had a partial view into the store and saw Watkins appear to purchase liquor at the counter. Watkins was arrested outside the store as he was leaving with a brown paper bag which contained a bottle of Thunderbird Wine. Cut-Rate Liquors and the clerk Dan Jones were issued citations for selling liquor to a person under the influence of liquor.

---

* This NITA Liquor Problem is used with the permission of the National Institute of Trial Advocacy (NITA). The terms "Officer Bier, Thunderbird Wine, Jackson & 7th Street, April 5th, Walter Watkins, and shoulders up" used in this publication are original to the Nita Liquor Commission v. Cut-Rate Liquor and Jones problem from Problems in Trial Advocacy by Donald H. Beskind and Anthony J. Bocchino, published by the National Institute of Trial Advocacy. The basis of the NITA Liquor problem and the specified terms are used here with permission.

NITA Liquor Commission
v.
Jones

The Facts

This case is a civil action brought by the Liquor Commission against Dan Jones and the Cut-Rate Liquor Store, for civil penalties, including possible revocation of Cut-Rate's liquor license. Investigator Bier is a typical investigator-police officer and has investigated many such incidents. Bier's official report appears on the next page along with a diagram of the scene.

Dan Jones and the Cut-Rate Liquor Store deny that Watkins was intoxicated on the evening of April 5 when he was in their store. Jones says that Watkins did not appear to be intoxicated when he observed Watkins in the store. Watkins was convicted of public intoxication at a prior trial. Watkins is not present for this Cut-Rate case.

1. Prepare to do a direct examination of Officer Bier for the government.

2. Prepare to do a cross examination of Officer Bier for the Defense.

Officer Bier's Report

NITA LIQUOR COMMISSION OFFICIAL REPORT

My partner Donald Smith and I are investigators for the Nita Liquor Commission. On the evening of April 5, at approximately 8:45 p.m., we were parked near the Cut-Rate Liquor Store when we observed an individual, later identified as Walter Watkins, attempting to cross 7th Street. Mr. Watkins was staggering and had great difficulty making it to the other side of the street. He stumbled and almost fell at the curb on the south side of 7th Street. He walked to the entrance of the Cut-Rate Liquor Store, and then paused for a few moments before he entered the store. The front of the store had a plate glass window with displays and advertising in it. From our car, we could see Mr. Watkins from the shoulders up through the window. We observed Mr. Watkins approach the counter and say a few words to the clerk, Dan Jones. A few minutes later, Watkins emerged from the store carrying a bottle of Thunderbird wine in a brown paper sack.

I stopped Mr. Watkins as he exited the store. I detected the odor of alcohol and administered a field sobriety test. I then arrested Watkins and issued him a citation for public intoxication, seized the wine, and issued a citation to Dan Jones and the Cut-Rate Liquor store for violation of H.R.S. 281-78 which contains the following language:

> No licensee nor its employees shall sell or furnish any liquor to any person at the time under the influence of liquor.

I have attached a diagram of the scene to this report.

Date: April 5   Time: 22:15

                                  signed J. Bier

Diagram of Cut-Rate Liquor Store Area

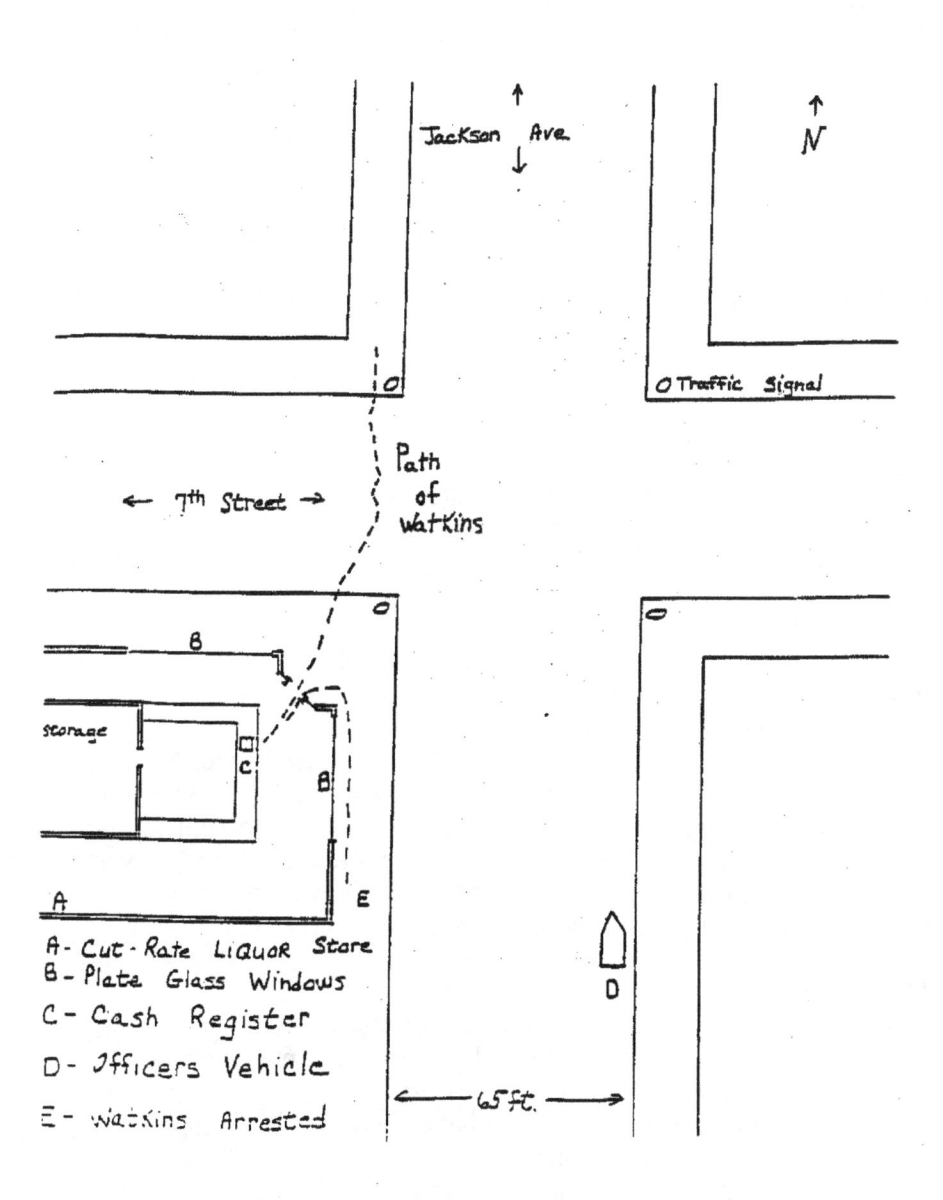

A - Cut-Rate Liquor Store
B - Plate Glass Windows
C - Cash Register
D - Officers Vehicle
E - Watkins Arrested

Laying Foundations

Photograph of a Scene

Introduce a photograph of Cut-Rate Liquor Store where the clerk and the liquor store were charged with selling liquor to an intoxicated person. R901(B)(1) (Testimony of a Witness with Knowledge)

Q: Officer Bier, where were you on the night of April 5?
A: Parked in an unmark car outside Cut-Rate Liquor Store.

Q: Let me show you what has been marked as Plaintiff's proposed exhibit # 1. <u>What is it?</u>
A: It is a photograph of Cut-Rate Liquor Store where I was parked on April 5th.

Q: <u>How do you know that?</u>
A: I was at the store that night. I recognize it. I took the photo.

Q: Is the photograph a <u>fair and accurate representation</u> of Cut-Rate Liquor store as it appeared <u>on April 5th</u>?
A: Yes.

Q: Your Honor, I offer the exhibit into evidence.

Enhancements/Additional Questions
- "Please describe the appearance of the store."
- "How many times have you seen the Cut-Rate Liquor Store?"
(Ask this question only if the witness has been to the store many times. However, being there once is enough for the foundation.) The witness can authenticate the photo even if the trial event was the only time the witness ever saw the store pictured in the photo

Additional Points:
- The photographer is not a necessary witness.
- The witness's personal knowledge of the contents of the photograph is all that is necessary.
- The witness does not have to have seen the photograph before coming to court.
- Print the photo and bring copies to court for the judge, jury, and opposing counsel.
- The photo could be a "Street view" from Google Maps that the witness has never seen before.

Diagram of the Scene

Demonstrative Evidence

Diagram from Officer Bier's Report

After some testimony about the events.

Q: Officer Bier, did you make a diagram of the scene that night? (Ans: Yes)

Q: Let me show you what has been marked as Plaintiff's proposed exhibit # 1. <u>What is it?</u> (Ans: My diagram)

Q: <u>How do you know that?</u> (Ans: I drew it. I remember it. That's my writing)

Q: Is it a <u>fair and accurate representation</u> of the intersection of Jackson and 7th Streets <u>on April 5th</u>? (Ans: Yes.)

Q: Is the proposed exhibit in the <u>same condition</u> as it was when you drew it on April 5th? (Ans: Yes.)

Q: Your Honor, I offer the exhibit into evidence.

Real Evidence

The Bottle of Thunderbird Wine Seized by Officer Bier

After some testimony about the events.

Q: Officer Bier, <u>what, if anything, did you recover</u> from Mr. Watkins that night?
(Ans: A bottle and a bag)

Q: Let me hand you what has been marked as Plaintiff's proposed exhibit # 2. <u>What is it?</u>
(Ans: The bottle and bag I seized from Watkins)

[If the bottle is in a bag, leave it in the bag. Have both the bottle and bag marked separately, e.g., Exhibits 1 and 2, A and B, 1 and 1A. Let the witness take the bottle out of the bag, like unwrapping a present. It will create some interest in what might be an otherwise boring trial.]

Q: <u>How do you know that?</u>
[Ans: My initials, in my handwriting, are on the bag along with the words "Cut-Rate Liquor" and "April 5."]

Q: Is the proposed exhibit # 2 <u>in the same or substantially the same condition</u> as it was when you recovered it from Watkins on April 5th?
(Ans: Generally, yes. However, some of the liquid was removed for testing for alcohol.)

Q: Your Honor, I offer the exhibit into evidence.

Offering A Contract into Evidence

Q: Mr. Johnny, I now want to ask you some questions about your dealings with Mr. King. In September, two years ago, did you have several conversations with Mr. King?
A: Yes. I did.

Q: What was the result of those conversations?
A: Mr. King and I entered into a contract for legal work.

Assume the exhibit has been pre-marked before the day of trial

Q: Let the record reflect that I am handing Mr. Johnny what has been pre-marked, as required by Court Rule, Plaintiff's proposed Exhibit # 1.
What is it Mr. Johnny?
A: It's the contract between me and Mr. King for the legal work that I was going to do for him.

Q: How do you know that? [Prepare the witness to answer this question]
A: I drafted this contract. I recognize it. That's my signature on it as well as Mr. King's.

Q: Is the contract in the same condition as it was two years when you both signed it.
A: Yes. There are no alterations to the contract.

Q: You Honor, I offer the exhibit into evidence

Laying Foundations

Refreshing Memory
(Anything can be used to refresh memory)

<u>Refreshing memory is almost always done on direct examination.
Impeachment is almost always done on cross examination.</u>

In the NITA case, assume witness Bier forgets some of Mr. Watkin's movements on the street. Refresh Bier's memory from his report. R612.

Q: Please describe Watkin's movements as he crossed 7th Street.
A: He staggered and had great difficulty getting to the other side of the street.

Q: Do you recall anything else about Watkins as he crossed the street.
A: Not really

Q: Officer Bier <u>did you make a report</u> in this case? A: Yes.

Q: Let me hand you what has been marked as Plaintiff's proposed exhibit # 3. <u>What is it?</u>
[Note: You are not going to introduce the document. Some judges might allow you to refresh memory without marking the exhibit, but the better practice is to have the document marked.]
A: My report.

Q: Please <u>read it to yourself</u>, especially the 4th and 5th lines.
(Note: You can focus the witness on what you want to witness to pay attention to.)

Q: <u>Let the record reflect that I am taking proposed exhibit # 3 away</u> from the Officer.
Now Officer Bier, is your memory refreshed?
A: Yes.

Q: What else do you now recall about how Watkins crossed 7th Street?
A: Watkins stumbled as he crossed 7th Street
(Discussion continued on the next page)

Recommendation: I suggest that you do not ask the witness, "Would anything refresh your memory." Just start refreshing. Isn't it strange to say, "Witness, I know you cannot remember, but can you remember anything that would help you remember what you have already forgotten?" Just refresh.

Additional points: The document used to refresh is not introduced into evidence. The witness' memory was refreshed. There is no need to introduce the document. There is no hearsay issue.

Writing Used to Refresh Memory

If a writing was used to refresh memory, R612 allows

> as a matter of right, if the document was used in court;
> with judge's discretion, if the document was used out of court

the opponent to:

1) see the writing in court,
2) inspect it
3) cross-examine on it, and
4) introduce portions of it (related to the testimony)

Simply: **Get, Inspect, Cross, Introduce.**

However, it would be very unusual for an opponent to introduce the document because most of the document would hurt the opponent's case. If the opponent wanted to introduce only portions of the document, the lawyer who used it to refresh memory would have an argument that under R106, in fairness other parts of the document should be considered at the same time.

Pa.R.E. 612. Writing or Other Item Used to Refresh a Witness's Memory
(a) **Right to Refresh Memory.** A witness may use a writing or other item to refresh memory for the purpose of testifying while testifying, or before testifying.
(b) **Rights of Adverse Party.**
    (1) If a witness uses a writing or other item to refresh memory while testifying, an adverse party is entitled to have it produced at the hearing, trial or deposition, to inspect it, to cross-examine the witness about it, and to introduce in evidence any portion that relates to the witness's testimony.
    (2) If a witness uses a writing or other item to refresh memory before testifying, and the court in its discretion determines it is necessary in the interests of justice, an adverse party is entitled to have it produced at the hearing, trial or deposition, to inspect it, to cross-examine the witness about it, and to introduce in evidence any portion that relates to the witness's testimony.
(c) **Rights of Producing Party.** If the producing party claims that the writing or other item includes unrelated matter, the court must examine it in camera, delete any unrelated portion, and order that the rest be delivered to the adverse party. Any portion deleted over objection must be preserved for the record.
(d) **Failure to Produce or Deliver.** If the writing or other item is not produced or is not delivered as ordered, the court may issue any appropriate order. But if the prosecution does not comply in a criminal case, the court must strike the witness's testimony or--if justice so requires--declare a mistrial, or the court may use contempt procedures.

Refreshing Memory with a Leading Question

(Using the same facts as the previous example)

Q: Do you recall anything else about Watkins as he crossed the street.
A: Not really

Q: Did he stumble and almost fall?

Opposing Lawyer: Objection: Leading

Q: I'll rephrase my question. What else do you recall about Watkins as he crossed the street.
A: Now I recall that he did stumble and almost fell crossing the street. I'm nervous. I forgot.

Note: The witness's credibility might have decreased somewhat because of the leading question, but the lawyer got the answer that was needed. The less important the information, the more likely leading will have little or no impact on your case.

Leading on Minor Issues When the Witness Has Gone Off Course

Q: What day of the week did this happen?
A: Tuesday.

Q: You said Tuesday. Did you actually mean Monday?
A: Oh right, sorry. It was Monday.

Recorded Recollection (Author's Rule)

Recorded recollection is a hearsay exception that allows <u>for reading into evidence</u> a statement that was made by a witness on the stand who can no longer recall the facts even after there has been attempts to refresh the witness's memory. Recorded recollection is <u>almost always done on direct examination</u> with a witness the lawyer has called to testify. This foundation is complicated and not intuitive.

In the NITA problem, assume that attempts to refresh the witness's memory did not work. Therefore, assume the previous question and answer were:

Q: What else do you now recall?
A: Sorry, I truly do not remember any more.

[Lawyer now moves into the foundation for Recorded Recollection, under R803(5).

Q: Let me again show you proposed exhibit # 3. That is your report of this incident, right? (Note: Leading is appropriate when establishing any foundations under R 104).
A: Yes

Q: You made that report when the incident was <u>fresh</u> in your mind?
A: Yes, just about an hour after the incident.

Q: Does the report <u>accurately reflect your knowledge</u> of the incident at the time of the incident?
A: Yes.

Q: Although you <u>once knew the details</u> of the incident and wrote them in your report, right now <u>you cannot now recall</u> the details of the incident well enough <u>to testify fully and accurately</u>, right?
A: Yes.

Q: Your honor, I would now <u>like to read</u> into the record those parts of the report that the witness no longer remembers. [Or, you could ask to have the witness read the portions of the report.]

(Discussion continued on the next page)

Pa.R.E. 803.1(3) Recorded Recollection A record that:
>((3) **Recorded Recollection of Declarant-Witness.** A memorandum or record made or adopted by a declarant-witness that:
>>(A) is on a matter the declarant-witness once knew about but now cannot recall well enough to testify fully and accurately;
>>(B) was made or adopted by the declarant-witness when the matter was fresh in his or her memory; and
>>(C) the declarant-witness testifies accurately reflects his or her knowledge at the time when made.
>
>If admitted, the memorandum or record may be read into evidence and received as an exhibit, but may be shown to the jury only in exceptional circumstances or when offered by an adverse party.

Additional Points: "Admission" into evidence comes from reading parts of the document into evidence. The document is not physically admitted by the proponent of the evidence. It cannot be taken into the jury room. Information in this hearsay document is admitted (heard) only once like oral testimony. Also, admitting information from a "Learned Treatise" under that hearsay exception R803(18) is a similar process in that the information from the treatise can only be read and not physically introduced.

Almost always, the witness was the author of the document used as the recorded recollection. Refreshing memory under R612 and recorded recollection are almost always done on direct examination. Witnesses are impeached on cross, not refreshed. You would not normally use recorded recollection on cross because almost all of the document goes against your client.

I think most lawyers prefer to read the recollection on direct examination themselves and not have the witness do it. By reading the recollection yourself, you can add what you consider the best tone, volume, pace, and emphasis for your case. Remember, when you use a past recollection recorded with your witness on direct, you cannot physically introduce the document into evidence. The proponent of the past recollection recorded "admits" the recollection by reading it, not physically admitting it.

Recorded recollection documents are not business records. Business records do get admitted into evidence. The difference is that if admitted, the evidence can be taken into the jury room and be consulted by the jury many times during deliberations.

A past recollection recorded includes all notes that a witness makes on any type of document. In evidence class, I pull out my wallet and show students all the recorded recollections that I have in my wallet (post-it notes, notes on business cards, notes on little scraps of paper, etc.) and any notes I have taken on my cell phone. Recorded Recollections and Statements in Learned Treatises, R803(18), are two types of hearsay documents which can only be read into evidence but not physically introduced, at least not by the proponent of a recorded recollection.

Business Records - Custodian of Records
(The actual hearsay exception is for "Regularly Conducted Activity," but is usually called "Business Records")

To prove that Cut-Rate Liquors had Thunderbird Wine in stock on April 5, a business record can be offered.

Q: Please state your name, occupation, and why you are here today.
A: I am Mr. Data, an employee of Cut-Rate Liquors. My duties at Cut-Rate include serving as the custodian of business inventory records for Cut-rate. I am here today pursuant to a subpoena to bring inventory records of Cut-Rate for April 5th.

Q: Did you bring with you today a copy of the Cut-Rate inventory records pertaining to Thunderbird wine for April 5th with you?
A: Yes.

Q: Do you know how Cut-Rate maintains its inventory records?
A: Yes.

Q: I show you what has been pre-marked as proposed exhibit # 1 and ask if you can identify what it is?
A: Yes, I can. Those are the Cute-Rate inventory records that I brought to court.

Q: Are those inventory records made by a person with <u>personal knowledge,</u> <u>at or near the time</u> the inventory is taken?
A: Yes.

Q: Are those records <u>kept in the course of a regularly conducted activity</u> of a business?
A: Yes.

Q: Is making those records a <u>regular practice</u> of Cut-Rate's business?
A: Yes.

Q: Your Honor, I offer the exhibit into evidence.

Publishing a Business Record: After being admitted, the business record can be "published" (which means it can be shown to the trier to fact). Depending on the judge's practice, the lawyer might be able to have the information from the record read to jury when it is admitted. If so, the Q & A could be:

Q: What do those records say about whether Cut-Rate had Thunderbird Wine in stock on April 5th?
A: "Thunderbird Wine, quantity 5," which means that Cut-Rate had five bottles of Thunderbird Wine in stock on April 5.

Remember, **business records are KRAP**. That acronym always gets my students' attention, and it helps them remember the foundation's components. **KRAP** – means:
Kept in the course,
Regular practice,
At or near the time,
Personal knowledge

The **custodian of records or other qualified witness** required by the business record evidence rule is often the owner of the business, a bookkeeper, or anybody who works in the business. They just have to be able to answer questions to provide the appropriate foundation.

Although it adds to the weight of the evidence to have a witness who has been employed for many years in the data collection of the business, that is not required. The custodian only needs to be able to testify to the foundation requirements. The custodian could have only been the custodian for one day, if they can credibly answer the foundational questions (although that fact might go to the weight of the evidence, but not its admissibility). The custodian does not have to be employed on the day the record was made.

I would prefer to use a self-authenticating business record. The custodian is open to a difficult cross.
"Do you know who made the business entry?" – Know their work history? Have they been disciplined? Know their accuracy? Are they still with the company? (Of course, you need a good faith basis).

Self-Authenticating Business Records

The Federal Rules of Evidence were amended in 2002 to allow business records to be self-authenticated by a written certification of the custodian or other qualified witness, which means that a witness does not have to appear in court. R902(11)(12). Many states have created statutes or forms to be used for the certification. An example of such a certification affidavit follows and many are available on the internet.

TEXAS FORM

Business Records Affidavit

FORM AR-1(08/10)   Tax Year _____   HCAD Account Number _____

This affidavit should be executed before a Notary Public or other official authorized to administer oaths and attached to the applicable business records. Please print or type.

Before me, the undersigned authority, personally appeared _____, who being by me duly sworn, deposed as follows:

My name is _____, I am of sound mind, capable of making this affidavit, and personally acquainted with the facts herein stated:

I am the custodian of the records of _____. Attached hereto are _____ pages of records from _____ (NAME OF BUSINESS). These said _____ pages of records are kept by _____ (NAME OF BUSINESS) in the regular course of business, and it was the regular practice of said entity for an employee or representative with knowledge of the act, event, condition, opinion, or diagnosis, recorded to make the record or to transmit information thereof to be included in such record; and the record was made at or near the time or reasonably soon thereafter. The records attached hereto are the original or exact duplicates of the original.

_____
Affiant's Signature

SWORN TO AND SUBSCRIBED before me on the ____ day of _____, _____.

(seal)

_____
Notary Public, State of Texas

_____
Notary's Printed Name

_____
My commission expires

Demonstrative Evidence Similar to the Real Item

Assume the bottle of Thunderbird wine in the Nita Liquor Commission case was dropped and broken after the contents had been tested in the lab and showed that it contained alcohol. At trial, a lawyer wants to introduce a bottle similar to the actual bottle of Thunderbird wine.

Q: Officer Bier, do you recognize proposed exhibit # 5?
A: Yes. I do.

Q: What is it?
A: It is a bottle like the one sold by Cut-Rate on the night of the incident.

Q: How do you know that?
A: I am a Liquor Commission Investigator. I am very familiar with Thunderbird wine as part of my job.

Q: "Is this bottle similar to the bottle you seized from Watkins on April 5?"
A: Yes.

Q: I offer the exhibit into evidence.

If there is a relevance objection to the "similar" bottle, the lawyer examining the witness needs to be ready to say, "Your honor, this bottle is relevant to show ...[some appropriate statement]." For example, the size and weight of the bottle suggests that Mr. Watkins could not have smuggled the bottle into the liquor store under his clothing. The similar bottle is not offered as the bottle that was sold that night, but it is being offered to prove something else, which is an example of limited admissibility under R105. The lawyer should not say, although it might be true, "My evidence professor always told us to introduce some physical evidence into the trial to wake up the trier of fact." [Such a statement offers a good trial strategy, but not a good response to the judge's question about relevance.]

Laying Foundations

Impeachment by Prior Written Inconsistent Statement
R613

Impeach Officer Bier from his report in the NITA problem, assuming Bier testified on direct exam, "I saw Watkins from the waist up inside the store."

Direct exam testimony was "...from the waist up...."
Report says "...from the shoulders up..."

Q: Today you testified on direct examination[1] that you could see Watkins inside the store from the waist up? (said in a disbelieving tone) (Commit to today's testimony.)
A: Yes.

Q: You made a written report in this case within a few hours of the incident? (Credit prior statement's reliability)
A: Yes.

Q: Let the record reflect that I am handing the witness proposed exhibit #x. Mr. Bier, proposed exhibit #x is the report you made within a couple of hours after the incident?
A: Yes.

Q: That is your signature on the report?
A: Yes

Q: Even though you said on direct examination that you could see Mr. Watkins inside the store from the waist up, doesn't it say right here in your report (pointing to it) that "we could see Mr. Watkins from the shoulders up through the window"?
A: Yes.

(Discussion continued on the next page)

---

[1] I suggest that you only use the phrase – "You testified on direct" – when you are going to impeach a witness with a prior statement. Do not use that phrase when you are asking questions about a real event that took place in your case. What happened on the day of the incident might be different that what a witness testified to on direct. You should keep the trier of fact's attention on the incident itself, not the testimony on direct – unless you are impeaching that direct testimony.

Stop. Ask no further questions on this topic. Don't say, "Are you lying today or were you lying then?" Such a question is probably argumentative and objectionable anyway. Do not argue with the witness or ask the witness to admit they are not telling the truth. Save the credibility argument for closing argument. In closing argument, you can make an argument without having the witness trying to explain away your impeachment.

Understand the difference between testimony about "waist up" and "shoulders up." If Officer Bier could see Mr. Watkins inside the store from the waist up, he could have seen the bottle of wine, the cash register, any money changing hands, and the wine bottle changing hands. All those facts go to showing that there was a sale of wine in violation of the statute. However, if the officer could only see inside the store at the shoulders up level, then he was not able to see any direct sale and the defense has a better argument.

Three impeaching steps here: commit; credit; and confront. 1) <u>Commit</u> the witness to the statement made on direct, 2) <u>credit</u> the prior out-of-court statement, and 3) <u>confront</u> the witness with the difference.

<u>By putting the conflicting statements in one sentence by using a dependent clause</u> ("Even though you said on direct examination that…"), <u>the trier of fact cannot miss the contradiction.</u> Some impeaching lawyers will emphasize certain words in their questions, so the trier of fact does not miss the inconsistency. For example, they would emphasize with tone, volume, pace, and any other nonverbal's, the words "waist up" and "shoulder up." The impeaching lawyer might want to make eye contact with the judge or the jury when emphasizing those words.

Additional questions that are sometimes asked, especially if it is a jury trial:
  Your prior statement was made closer in time to the event than your statement today?
  Your memory was better at the earlier time?
  You have had training on how to write reports?
  You know that your supervisor will read your reports?
  You know that you are evaluated on, and perhaps even promoted or demoted based on the quality of your reports?

Impeachment by Omission

Assume that <u>Bier testified on direct exam</u>, "As I was sitting in my car watching Watkins <u>inside the store, I saw that Watkins stumble and almost fall as he approached the counter.</u>" However, Officer Bier's report does not say that Watkins stumbled and almost fell inside the store. In fact, the report indicates that the officer could only see Watkins from the shoulders up as he approached the counter. Impeachment by omission - meaning that the witness testified in court to something that was not in the report - it is a little harder to accomplish than a direct prior inconsistent statement, but it is still very doable.

Q: <u>You testified on direct</u> examination that you saw Mr. Watkins stumble and almost fall as he approached the counter inside from the store? (Credit prior statement's reliability)
A: Yes.

Q: You made a written report in this case within an hour of the incident, right?
A: Yes.

Q: I am handing the witness proposed exhibit #x.
This is the report you made within a couple of hours after the incident, isn't it?
A: Yes.

Q: That is your signature on the report, isn't that true?
A: Yes

Q: <u>Even though you said on direct examination</u> that you saw Mr. Watkins <u>stumble and almost fall</u> as he approached the counter <u>inside</u> the store, <u>nowhere</u> in this report that you prepared <u>does it state</u> that you saw Watkins stumble and almost fall <u>inside</u> the store, does it? [If the witness takes time to look for it in the report, give them as much time as they want to take.
A: No, it doesn't say that.

The report says nothing about Watkins' behavior in the store. Behavior in the store is critical to proving that defendant Jones knew that Watkins was intoxicated.

Additional questions beyond the bare-bones foundation.
Lawyer could build up the report, for example:

> "You try to put everything that is important in the report, right?"
> "They taught you to do that in the department training, right?"

The potential re-direct examination:
If it were my witness who was impeached, my redirect would go something like this:

Q: Officer, how do you explain what seems to be an inconsistency between your direct testimony that Watkins stumbled inside the store and your report, which does not mention Watkins stumbled inside the store?

A: [Perhaps the best answer would be] I can't put everything into the report. But I clearly remember that he stumbled inside the store.

Impeachment by Inconsistent Oral Deposition

Assume the same factual inconsistency of testimony on direct examination that Mr. Watkins stumbled inside the store, but this time also assume that Officer Bier gave an oral deposition under oath and gave an answer that did not mention any stumbling inside the store.

After laying a foundation which would include the procedures involved in the deposition, such as:
- You came to my office?
- You took an oath to tell the truth?
- I told you that if you didn't understand the question, you should tell me you don't understand?
- You had an opportunity to review and correct the transcript some weeks after the deposition?
- After you read the typed deposition, you signed the deposition as being accurate?

then complete the impeachment by reading the questions that were asked and the answers that were given at the deposition.

The impeaching sequence could go something like this:

Q: Even though you said on direct that Watkins stumbled and almost fell in the store when he was at the counter, at your deposition weren't you asked this question, and didn't you give this answer:

> Q: Now Officer Bier, how was Watkins walking when he was inside the store?
> A: I can't say for sure. My view into the store was obstructed.

A: Yes, that is what it says.

You want to confine your questions to what the witness said at the deposition, not what the witness remembers now. Your opponent will no doubt do redirect examination to try to rehabilitate the witness.

Impeachment by Inconsistent Oral Deposition - Short Form

On direct examination, the witness said, "The light was green." You want to impeach with the witness' deposition that says, "The light was red."

Q: On direct examination you said the light was green?
A: Yes.

Q: Even though on direct examination you said that the light was green, at the deposition weren't you asked the following question, and didn't you give the following answer?
Q: What color was the light?
A: The light was red.
A: Yes.

Laying Foundations

Impeachment by Inconsistent Oral Deposition - Long Form

On direct examination, the witness said, "The light was green." You want to impeach with the witness' deposition that says, "The light was red."

Highlight the Inconsistency
Q. On direct examination you said the light was green. [A: Yes]
Q. There is no question in your mind about that? [A: No question.]

Lock the Witness into The Testimony (you can omit this step)
Q. Have you ever said anything different? [No]
Q. Are you sure it was green? [Yes]
Q. Isn't it true that the light was in fact red? [No]

Build Up the Impeaching Document
Q. You remember coming to my office last year to answer some questions?
Q. You came for a deposition on July 11, last year?
Q. I asked you questions, and you gave me answers, isn't that right?
Q. Your lawyer sat next to you while you answered?
Q. A court reporter took down your answers?
Q. That reporter gave you an oath to tell the truth?
Q. You agreed to tell the truth?
Q. After that deposition, the Q's and A's were typed up and you had a chance to read it over?
Q. After making sure it was correct, you signed it didn't you?
Q. This is your signature, isn't it?
Q. This deposition was just four months after the accident?
Q. Even though on direct examination you said that the light was green, at the deposition weren't you asked the following question, and didn't you give the following answer?
    Q: What color was the light?
    A: The light was red.

Impeachment by Inconsistent Oral Statement
(Assuming only the cross-examining lawyer heard the inconsistent statement)

Assume that although Bier testified on direct exam that "Watkins stumbled and almost fell inside the store," Bier was overheard outside the courtroom say to a person who is not available to testify, "I never really saw Watkins stumble inside the store." However, only the lawyer for Cut-Rate Liquor heard Bier's statement.

This is an inconsistent oral statement. Unlike most inconsistent statements, this one was <u>not made prior</u> to the in-court testimony on direct exam. <u>This statement was made after</u> the in-court testimony.

This fact pattern presents a special problem if the lawyer was the only person who overhead the statement. If Bier denies making the statement, the cross-examiner does not have a witness who could be called to the stand to complete the impeachment of Bier. So, if no one other that the lawyer overhead the statement, what can the lawyer do? The lawyer certainly cannot testify in this case.

A suggestion would be to handle this problem by being as detailed as possible during the questioning leading up to the impeaching question. If the trier of fact believes the details, the trier of fact might believe that Bier also made the final statement ("I never saw him stumble inside the store.").

Detailed questioning
Q: During the break, you went outside the courtroom, didn't you?
Q: And you sat on the bench outside?
Q: You sat next to a man wearing a blue shirt, right?
Q: And the two of you had a conversation?
Q: You talked for about 5 minutes, right?
Q: "Even though you said on direct exam in court just 30 minutes ago that Watkins stumbled and almost fell in the store when he was at the counter, didn't you say to a man on a bench outside this courtroom just 10 minutes ago, "I never really saw Watkins stumble inside the store?"

Learned Treatises:
Use on Direct Exam to Support Your Expert
FRE 803(18) – Hearsay Exception

> **Pennsylvania is one of 12 states that does NOT have a learned treatise hearsay exception. The direct exam below is NOT permitted in Pennsylvania courts**

After an expert testifies that it is not possible to determine if the plaintiff's epileptic seizures are caused by the plaintiff's auto accident, the following questioning takes place to use a learned treatise to support the expert's opinion. This is an example of using a "paper expert," or said another way, getting the opinion of two experts but only calling one as a witness.

Q: Dr. Rosenberg, are you familiar with the text called Medicine written by Dr. Mark Fishman?
A: Yes

Q: Let me show you proposed exhibit #1. What is it?
A: It is the book called Medicine written by Dr. Mark Fishman.

Q: Is it a recognized as a reliable authority in the field of medicine?
A: Yes

Q: What does the Fishman text say about the causes of epileptic seizures?
A: On page 135, Fishman says that a cause is found for seizures in less than 25% of the cases.

Using a learned treatise as a hearsay exception can only done by reading the treatise to the trier of fact, but not by physically introducing the treatise into evidence. FRE 803(18). <u>Pennsylvania has not adopted this rule.</u>

(Discussion continued on the next page)

Although Pennsylvania courts have not adopted FRE 803(18), see Aldridge *v.* Edmunds, 750 A.2d 292 (Pa. 2000), where they have permitted, subject to appropriate restraint by the trial court, limited identification of textual materials (and in some circumstances their contents) on direct examination to permit an expert witness to fairly explain the basis for his reasoning. See, Aldridge v. Edmunds, 750 A.2d 292 (Pa. 2000) showing in question and answer form, the permitted use of learned treatises on direct examination.

FRE 803(18). Exceptions to the Rule Against Hearsay — Regardless of Whether the Declarant Is Available as a Witness
The following are not excluded by the rule against hearsay, regardless of whether the declarant is available as a witness:
(18) Statements in Learned Treatises, Periodicals, or Pamphlets.
A statement contained in a treatise, periodical, or pamphlet if:
  (A) the statement is <u>called to the attention of an expert</u> witness on cross-examination or relied on by the expert on direct examination; and
  (B) the publication is established as a <u>reliable authority</u> by the expert's admission or testimony, by another expert's testimony, or by judicial notice.
If admitted, the statement may be <u>read</u> into evidence <u>but not received</u> as an exhibit.

3 Key Points for Using the Learned Treatise

To use a learned treatise on either direct or cross-examination, under R803(18)
1) there must be an expert <u>on the witness stand,</u>
2) the treatise has been established as a <u>reliable authority</u>, and
3) the statement may be <u>only read</u> into the record, but the treatise cannot be physically introduced into evidence.

Learned Treatises: Use on Cross to Attack the Opposing Expert FRE 803(18) – Hearsay Exception

After establishing that Mark Fishman's text called "Medicine" is a reliable authority in the field of medicine, either by your expert, or by your opponent's expert, or by judicial notice (Note: judges seldom take judicial notice on this subject), the lawyer below uses the learned treatise on cross examination to contradict the opposing party's expert witness. A statement in a treatise can be used to impeach the opponent's expert and as substantive evidence (meaning for the truth of the statement – this is a hearsay exception).

Q: Dr. Barron, you testified during your direct examination that Mr. Fulbright's epilepsy was caused by the auto accident, right?
A: Yes.

Q: Dr., there is no medical evidence that Mr. Fulbright showed any clinical evidence of brain injury immediately after the incident is there?
A: That's correct.

Q: And no evidence of a skull fracture?
A: That's also correct.

Q: And no evidence of bloody spinal fluid, right?
A: Correct again.

Q: Dr., doesn't the text called, Medicine, written by Mark Fishman, indicate on page 132 that the four symptoms most commonly found with epileptic seizures are 1) loss of consciousness, 2) clinical evidence of brain injury immediately after the incident, 3) skull fracture, and 4) bloody spinal fluid?
A: Yeah, Fishman does say that.

Q: Your Honor, no further questions.

Voicemail, Phone Conversations, Recorded Phone Conversations

There is nothing special about the identification of a telephone call. Authentication for voice identification is covered in the R901(b)(5)&(6).

Do you know X?

How do you know X?

How long have you known X?

Have you ever spoken with X on the phone?

How often have you spoken with X on the phone?

On [the day in question] did you have a phone conversation with X?

Who initiated that call?

[If **your** witness initiated the call]

> How did you make the call? [Ans: used contacts list on cell phone; used recent call list on cell phone; used landline]
>
> Was their name already in your cell phone from previous calls to them?
>
> Did you recognize the voice when your call was answered?
>
> Who were you talking to?

(Continued on next page)

[If the **other party** initiated the call]

> Could you tell who was calling you?
>
> How could you tell who was calling you? [Name appeared on my cell phone]
>
> Why did their name appear in your cell phone? [I had name in my contacts list from many previous calls]
>
> Who was on the phone when you answered the call? [The defendant]
>
> How did you know that? [We have talked many times before. I recognized his voice.]

What did he say during that call?

Digital Evidence
Electronically Stored Information – ESI

Electronically Stored Information (EIS) includes emails, text messages, websites, fax, social media, computer printouts, and other digital records. Although we evidence professors will tell you that the classic rules of evidence, created before cell phones, computers, and the Internet, are more than adequate for the new digital world, some people doubt it.

Yet truly, introducing digital evidence in court still does apply the same basic HARROWing principles found in all evidence codes –
H = Hearsay;
A= Authentication;
R= R401 relevancy (sometime called "logical relevancy);
R=R403 (sometimes called "legal Relevancy);
OW = Original Writings (traditionally known as Best Evidence).

The same rules of evidence apply to ESI as they do to paper and physical evidence. The most challenging foundational issues for digital evidence are establishing: 1) who created the digital evidence (the author), and 2) has it been altered?

A Variety of Standards
Different standards have developed in various jurisdictions for authenticating digital evidence.

The Texas courts, and probably most jurisdictions, use an authentication standard identical to the standard used for traditional forms of evidence – "evidence sufficient to support a finding (R 901). The Texas standard can be thought of and remembered by the state's placement on a map – it is a lower standard.

However, the Maryland courts, and a few others, have developed a higher standard – like Maryland's placement on a map. Maryland courts seem to require that the proponent of digital evidence prove that the digital evidence has not been altered or hacked, it comes from a certain source, and that no one other than the owner could have used the electronic device to send or post the message. This view of EIS authentication is concerned about "voodoo information taken from the Internet." It creates a standard that can seldom be met. However, in more recent cases Maryland courts have backed away from that high standard and seem now to favor a more traditional approach for authenticating digital evidence.

The Grimm, Joseph & Capra article, Best Practices for Authenticating Digital Evidence 69 Baylor L.R. 1 (2017) is a great source for understanding factors in authenticating digital evidence. That article presents an overview of how Rules of Evidence 104(a) and 104(b) interact in the authentication process and argues that digital evidence should be authenticated requiring only evidence
"sufficient to support a finding," - which is a low standard.
The authors offer the opinion that,
> "Generally speaking, it will be a rare case in which an item of digital evidence cannot be authenticated."

The article covers various ways to authenticate digital evidence. Most helpful will be the examples of various types of circumstantial evidence that would qualify as "distinctive characteristics" under R901(b)(4). Additional, less frequently used methods of authenticating evidence are also covered, such as, personal knowledge of a witness, business records (in some email situations), jury comparison, and production in discovery.

> **The comment to Pa.R.E. 901(b)(11) reads:**
>
> Pa.R.E. 901(b)(11) has no counterpart in the Federal Rules of Evidence. "Digital evidence," as used in this rule, is intended to include a communication, statement, or image existing in an electronic medium. This includes emails, text messages, social media postings, and images. The rule illustrates the manner in which digital evidence may be attributed to the author.
>
> **The proponent of digital evidence is not required to prove that no one else could be the author. Rather, the proponent must produce sufficient evidence to support a finding that a particular person or entity was the author.** *See* **Pa.R.E. 901(a).**
>
> Direct evidence under Pa.R.E. 901(b)(11)(A) may also include an admission by a party-opponent.
>
> Circumstantial evidence of identifying content under Pa.R.E. 901(b)(11)(B)(i) may include self-identification or other distinctive characteristics, including a display of knowledge only possessed by the author. Circumstantial evidence of content may be sufficient to connect the digital evidence to its author.
>
> Circumstantial evidence of ownership, possession, control, or access to a device or account alone is insufficient for authentication of authorship of digital evidence under Pa.R.E. 901(b)(11)(B)(ii). *See, e.g., Commonwealth v. Mangel*, 181 A.3d 1154, 1163 (Pa. Super. 2018) (social media account bearing defendant's name, hometown, and high school was insufficient to authenticate the online and mobile device chat messages as having been authored by defendant). However, this evidence is probative in combination with other evidence of the author's identity.
>
> Expert testimony may also be used for authentication purposes. *See, e.g., Commonwealth v. Manivannan*, 186 A.3d 472 (Pa. Super. 2018).
>
> There are a number of statutes that provide for authentication or identification of various types of evidence. *See, e.g.*, 42 Pa.C.S. § 6103 (official records within the Commonwealth); 42 Pa.C.S. § 5328 (domestic records outside the Commonwealth and foreign records); 35 P.S. § 450.810 (vital statistics); 42 Pa.C.S. § 6106 (documents filed in a public office); 42 Pa.C.S. § 6110 (certain registers of marriages, births and burials records); 75 Pa.C.S. § 1547(c) (chemical tests for alcohol and controlled substances); 75 Pa.C.S. § 3368 (speed timing devices); 75 Pa.C.S. § 1106(c) (certificates of title); 42 Pa.C.S. § 6151 (certified copies of medical records); 23 Pa.C.S. § 5104 (blood tests to determine paternity); 23 Pa.C.S. § 4343 (genetic tests to determine paternity).

Distinctive Characteristics and Circumstantial Evidence Used to Authenticate Emails and Text Messages as having been sent by a particular person or as having been received by a particular person

There are many possible ways to use circumstantial evidence to qualify as "distinctive characteristics" to authenticate Electronically Stored Information (ESI) under R901(b)(4) Distinctive Characteristics and the Like. Appearance, contents, substance, internal patterns, or other distinctive characteristics of the item taken together with all the circumstances are almost endless.

The Grimm, Joseph & Capra article offers many extremely valuable suggestions about circumstantial evidence which can be considered "distinctive characteristics" and used to authenticate digital evidence under R901(b)(4).

For example, when laying the foundation <u>for an email or text</u>, consider:
   1) information <u>in or about</u> the email or text
   2) information <u>outside</u> the email or text itself <u>that leads back to the author</u>
   3) <u>forensic</u> information, and
   4) information <u>outside</u> the email or text itself <u>indicating receipt of the message.</u>

Factors suggested by Grimm, Joseph, and Capra used to authenticate authorship or receipt of a message include:

   1) information in or about the email or text, such as:
      - the email address, email signature, a nickname, a screen name, initials, a moniker, the author's customary use of emoji or emoticons, a writing style (including phrases and abbreviations frequently used by the author), referring to facts only the author or small group of people would know about, facts uniquely tied to the author, information about the author's family, photos of the author, items of importance to the author such as a car or a pet, and other such information

2) information outside the email or text itself that leads back to the author, such as:
- the email was part of a chain or series of emails from the same person, the claimed author told the witness to expect an email from the author, the author orally repeats its content soon after the email is sent, the author discusses the contents of the email with the third party, the author leaves a voicemail substantially of the same content, and other such information

3) forensic information, such as:
- an email's hash values or testimony from a forensic witness that the email came from a particular device at a particular time, and other such information

4) information outside the email or text itself indicating receipt of the message, such as:
- a reply was received by the sender that came from the recipient, later conduct of the recipient reflects knowledge of the contents of the sent message, later communication of the recipient reflects knowledge of the message, and the message was received and accessed on an electronic device in the possession of the recipient, and other such information.

Presenting the Digital Evidence from a Cell Phone in Court

- Print the page from the phone and use the printout in court.
- If a photo comes from a cell phone, attach the picture to an email, and then print from a computer.
- Screenshot the information (picture, text message, email, social media post), email it, then print from a computer.

Self-Authentication for Digital Evidence

Recent amendments to the Federal Rules of Evidence allow for self-authentication of certified records, see FRE 902(13)&(14), <u>as does</u> similar recent amendments to the **Pennsylvania Rules of Evidence**

Digital Evidence and Self-Authentication

Pa.R.E. 902 Self-authentication
(11) Certified Domestic Records of a Regularly Conducted Activity.
The original or a copy of a domestic record that meets the requirements of Rule 803(6)(A)-(C), as shown by a certification of the custodian or another qualified person that complies with Pa.R.C.P. No. 76. Before the trial or hearing, the proponent must give an adverse party reasonable written notice of the intent to offer the record--and must make the record and certification available for inspection--so that the party has a fair opportunity to challenge them.

> Many states have created forms for self-authentication of business records or have court rules which cover certifications for business records.

FRE 902(13) (Added to FRE Dec. 2017)
(13) Certified Records Generated by an Electronic Process or System. A record generated by an electronic process or system that produces an accurate result, as shown by a <u>certification of a qualified person that complies with the certification requirements of Rule 902(11) or (12).</u> The proponent must also meet the notice requirements of Rule 902(11).
[JB: covers text messages, cell phone photos, GPS data, and other ESI]

> Note: **Pennsylvania <u>has</u>** adopted this rule.
> The following 10 states have this rule:
> Alabama, Arizona, Illinois, Maryland, Mississippi,
> North Dakota, Ohio, Pennsylvania, Utah, and Wyoming

FRE 902(14) Certified Data Copied from an Electronic Device, Storage Medium, or File. Data copied from an electronic device, storage medium, or file, if authenticated by a process of digital identification, as shown by a <u>certification of a qualified person that complies with the certification requirements of Rule 902(11) or (12)</u>. The proponent also must meet the notice requirements of Rule 902(11).

> Note: **Pennsylvania <u>has</u>** adopted this rule.
> The following 10 states have this rule:
> Alabama, Arizona, Illinois, Maryland, Mississippi,
> North Dakota, Ohio, Pennsylvania, Utah, and Wyoming

Email – Witness is the Sender (Outgoing Email)

Q: How did you notify Cut-Rate about …
A: I sent an email to Dan Jones

Q: What email address did you use?
A: DJones@Cutrate.com

Q: How do you know that was the correct address?
A: He and I have email back and forth for a few months, and all of his emails to me came from that email address

Q: Let me show you what has been marked as plaintiff's proposed exhibit #1.

Q: What is it? (A printout of the email I sent to Jones that day.).

Q: How do you know that? (I wrote it. I remember it. It was in my "sent mail" folder.)

Q: Your Honor I offer the exhibit into evidence.

Email – Witness is the Recipient (Incoming Email)

Do you know Dan Jones?

How do you know him?

Are you familiar with the email address DJones@Cutrate.com?

Have you received emails from Dan Jones in the past?

Have you sent emails to Dan Jones at that address?

Has he responded to your emails from that email address?

Is that email address in your email contacts?

In late April, did you receive an email from Dan Jones about selling liquor?

Did you recognize email address as being from Dan Jones?

I am handing you what has been marked as proposed exhibit #7. You recognize it?

What is it? (A: The email from Dan Jones)

Why would you say that's an email from Dan Jones? [provides information about distinctive characteristics of this email]

How did you get a paper copy of this email? (A: I printed it out.)

Is this a true and accurate printout of that email?

Your Honor, I offer the proposed exhibit into evidence.

> [The email reads: "I might be getting fired. They caught me selling booze to drunks again."]

Text Message
Received by Witness

Do you know Y?

Do you communicate with Y on a regular basis?

In what ways to you communicate with Y?

Did you receive a text message from the Y [recently; on or about _ date, on the topic of …, etc.]?

Would you recognize a printout of the message if you were to see it again?

Let me show you what has been marked as proposed exhibit # 1. Do you recognize it?

What is it? [Ans: A screenshot from my cell phone]

How do you know that this is a message from Y? [It is similar to other messages I have received from Y in that …]

How did it appear when it arrived on your phone? [Showed up under the name and with the picture I had previously assigned to Y]

What other distinctive characteristics did you notice about the message? [provide as many as distinctive characteristics possible]

Is it a fair and accurate representation of the text message you received [recently; on or about _ date, on the topic of visiting your son, etc.]?

Has it been altered in any way?

I would like to enter the proposed exhibit into evidence

Social Media
Facebook, Instagram, Snapchat, Twitter, and other Posts

Do you know B?

How long have you known him?

Are you familiar with Facebook?

Does B have a Facebook account?

Have you seen posts by B on his Facebook account in the past?

How do you know that B made those posts? [provide distinctive characteristics]

Have you seen a posting on B's Facebook account about [the matter in question]?

Let the record reflect that I am handing you what has been marked as proposed exhibit 12 and ask if you can identify it?

What is it?

Is that a screenshot of the Facebook posting by B about ___?

What day did you take the screenshot?

Is it a true and accurate screenshot of that posting?

Is the post still on B's account? [Ask this question only if it is currently on the account.]

I offer the proposed exhibit into evidence.

Internet Website – Web Posting

Did you visit Professor John Barkai's webpage? [Yes]

How did you access it? [Googled "John Barkai" on my phone]

How did you find his page?
   Ans: I clicked on the link that said "Prof. John Barkai Homepage."

What did you find when you clicked on that link for the homepage?
   Ans: I found his list of courses and other posts.

Did you click on any particular link?
   Ans: I clicked Hawaii Rules of Evidence (HRE) Book Page

What did you find on that page when you clicked on it?
   A: I found a link to buy from Amazon a copy of this Rules of Evidence Handbook.

Let me show you what's been marked as proposed exhibit # 14. Can you identify it?
   A: Yes. It's a screenshot of that webpage with instructions about how to buy a copy of this book from Amazon.

Was that screenshot a print of the page from his website?
   A: Yes, I printed it myself.

Is this exhibit a fair and accurate copy of that webpage? [Yes]

Has this exhibit of the screenshot been altered or otherwise change from the image on your phone in any way? [No]

I offer the exhibit into evidence.

Fax – Incoming

Does your office have a fax machine?

Do you send outgoing faxes?

Do you receive incoming faxes?

Have you received purchase orders from the defendant by fax in the past?

Let me show you plaintiff's proposed exhibit # 27 and ask if you can identify it? [A: Yes. I can]

What is it? [A: A fax I received about six months ago from the defendant]

Why do you say this fax came from the defendant?
A: There are number of factors in addition to the document being written on the defendant's letterhead stationery. The fax is signed by the head of defendant's purchasing department, and I am familiar with her signature from our past dealings. Further, imprinted on the bottom of this fax sheet is the fax number for the defendant's company, and I have faxed prior documents to the defendant by using that number. Finally, the document relates to the purchase of some equipment that I had discussed with the defendant's head of purchasing just a few hours before the fax arrived at my office.

Is this document in the same or substantially the same condition as it was when you received it? [A: Yes, it is exactly the same.]

There have been no alterations or changes? [A: None whatsoever.]

Your Honor, I move that this proposed exhibit be admitted into evidence.

Laying Foundations

Expert Opinions

> Pennsylvania follows the Frye ("general acceptance") standard for expert opinions. See Comment to Pa.R.E. 702

> **Admissibility of Expert Testimony.**
> The majority of states have explicitly adopted the Daubert (FRE702) standard.
> A minority of states use either the Frye ("general acceptance") standard or some combination of Daubert and Frye standards.
> Additionally, "general acceptance" is part of the Daubert standard.

Four Part Expert Opinion Foundation and Testimony

1. Elicit the background and qualifications of the expert
2. Tender or offer the witness as expert in a particular field (e.g., 'general medicine.")
   – Opponent is allowed to voir dire (test qualifications by cross examination limited to the expert's qualifications, but not the facts of this case)
3. Offer the expert's opinion or conclusion (to a particular standard such as "reasonable medical certainty") FRE 702
4. Offer the basis for opinion FRE703
   – Including reasonable reliance on inadmissible evidence
   – Disclosure of inadmissible evidence?

Three Simple Questions

> 1) Q: "Do you have an opinion as to whether...
> 2) Q: "What is that opinion?"
> 3) Q: "How did you reach that opinion?
>   A: [including inadmissible information reasonably relied upon by experts in the particular field, FRE 703]

How to Start
   The expert witness examination normally starts with questions to establish the witness' qualifications to testify as an expert.

Topics for Background and Qualifications of an Expert:
   - formal education, work experience, number of previous times retained, qualified, and testified as an expert, in which courts, on-the-job training, non-degree training courses, publications in the field, teaching in the field, memberships in related professional associations, and any other topics relevant to showing the person is an expert.

Tender / Offer

After presenting the expert's background and qualifications, in jurisdictions where the judge must "certify" or "find" that the witness is an expert and is to permitted to testify as an expert, the lawyer presenting the expert then "tenders" or "offers" the witness to the judge as an expert, stating the field of expertise.

"I offer/tender Mr. X as an expert in the field of…"

"I ask the court to certify Ms. Y as an expert in the field of …"

Can you call the expert an "expert?"

After any voir dire (a limited cross examination to test the qualifications of the witness) by opposing counsel and objections, the judge rules on whether the expert can continue to testify as an expert. Some courts do not allow the lawyer to use the word "expert" to refer to the expert witness. but the judge is still changed with the responsibility of determining if the witness is qualified as an expert. Yet no one uses the word "expert" in front of lay fact finders. The apparent reason for such a practice is, as explained below.

The 2000 Advisory Committee Notes to the amendment to Federal Rule of Evidence 702 says, in part:

> "…The use of the term "expert" in the Rule does not, however, mean that a jury should actually be informed that a qualified witness is testifying as an "expert." Indeed, there is much to be said for a practice that prohibits the use of the term "expert" by both the parties and the court at trial. Such a practice "ensures that trial courts do not inadvertently put their stamp of authority" on a witness's opinion, and protects against the jury's being "overwhelmed by the so-called 'experts'."

More Tenders/Offers of the expert

"We believe that Mr. Taylor <u>should be permitted</u> to offer his opinions in this case."

"I <u>tender</u> Dr. Barron as an expert in the field of family medicine and request that she be allowed to testify as such.

"I <u>offer</u> Dr. Rosenberg as an expert in the field of neurology."

"Judge, we ask that the court <u>accept</u> Dr. Shigeta as an expert in civil engineering."

Offering the Opinion

Traditionally, the opinion is delivered in a two questions sequence:
Q1: Do you have an opinion as ….?
A: Yes
Q2: What is that opinion?

"Do you have an opinion, <u>within a reasonable degree of scientific certainty</u>, as to the time of death of Ms. X?"

"Do you have an opinion, <u>to a reasonable degree of medical probability</u>, as to whether the motorcycle accident caused Mr. Fulbright's epilepsy?"

"Do you have an opinion, <u>to a reasonable degree of engineering certainty</u>, as to whether the XXX caused the bridge to fail?"

"Do you have an opinion whether Mr. X suffered a brain damage as a result of the fight?"

Standards for Stating an Expert's Opinion

There are no minimum standards under R702 describing how "good" an expert's opinion must be to be stated in court. By case law, some courts and jurisdictions require that the standard must be stated to a
 "reasonable degree of [medical] <u>certainty</u>," or a
 "reasonable degree of [scientific] <u>probability.</u>"
Other jurisdictions simply allow an expert to state an opinion without any specific qualification.
 "What did your examination reveal?"

The above standards of "certainty" and "probability" are vague and rather unhelpful standards to a lay jury or courts-martial member who might be able to understand percentages, but who is given no guidance to the certainty or probability. Do those standards mean 51%, 65%, 75%, 85%, 95%, etc.? "Preponderance of the evidence" does have an associated percentage (50%+), but terms such as "sufficient to support a finding," "clear and convincing," "beyond a reasonable doubt," as well as "certainty" and "probability" do not. Simply, use whatever standard your judge and jurisdiction require.

In an attempt to be persuasive, some lawyers ask the experts questions like:

"How positive are you of your opinion?"
"What is the degree of your certainty?"

Inadmissible Information Reasonably Relied Upon
Experts can base their opinions on hearsay and other inadmissible evidence. R703 says in part:

"If experts in the particular field would reasonably rely on those kinds of facts or data in forming an opinion on the subject, they need not be admissible for the opinion to be admitted."

You should have in your tool chest of questions this question.
"Is that the type of information reasonably relied upon by experts in your field?

Remember

Whoever has the Biggest, Most Qualified Expert Might Win
Because opposing parties often have opposing experts, who have reached opposing conclusions, the advocacy principle is for you to try to present a more qualified and more credible expert than your opponent's expert. If "your" expert's testimony and conclusions are believed on the issue that the experts are testifying about, you are more likely to win your case.

Pennsylvania is a Frye jurisdiction, not Daubert
Pennsylvania continues to use the Frye test as seen in Pa.R.Evid 702 Testimony by Expert Witnesses, which reads in part – "the expert's methodology is generally accepted in the relevant field."

History and Restyling of the Federal Rules of Evidence

The Pennsylvania Rules of Evidence are based upon, and in many parts very similar to, the Federal Rules of Evidence (FRE), which were adopted in 1975. Approximately 46 states have adopted evidence codes, by statute or court rule, which are patterned on the FRE. The states without FRE based evidence codes are California, Kansas, Missouri, and New York. The California Evidence Code took effect in 1965 and is quite different in structure than any other state evidence code.

Although most states modeled their evidence rules after the FRE, almost every state has some evidence provisions which are different from the federal rules and some states have very significant differences.

The FRE were "restyled" in 2011 to
> "make them more easily understood and to make style and terminology consistent throughout the rules. These changes are intended to be stylistic only. There is no intent to change any result in any ruling on evidence admissibility.... The [Restyling] Committee made special efforts to reject any purposed style improvement that might result in a substantive change in the application of a rule." --- See Restyled Rules Committee Note for Restyled Rules of Evidence.

At least thirteen (13) states have restyled their rules of evidence: Arizona (2012), Delaware (2017), Idaho (2018), Indiana (2013), Iowa (2017), Maine (2015), Mississippi (2016), New Hampshire (2017), Pennsylvania (2013), South Dakota (2016), Texas (2014), Utah (2012), and West Virginia (2014).

Teaching Evidence Since 4 B.C.

Art by Dan Mazanec

John Barkai has been teaching evidence since 4 B.C. – that is 4 years "Before Computers" were used at the University of Hawaii Law School. His major criminal trial practice experience was in 1972-1973 in Detroit, and included jury trials on charges for Murder, Criminal Sexual Conduct (Statutory Rape at the that time), Armed Robbery, Assault, and CCW (Carrying A Concealed Weapon). He did not use the federal rules of evidence at that time. No one did. The Federal Rules did not go into effect until July 1975, by which time he was a fulltime law professor. For the past 50 years, he has taught a criminal clinic in which his students try traffic and misdemeanor cases under the state student practice rule.

Books by John Barkai

Federal Rules of Evidence Handbook with Common Objections & Evidentiary Foundations

Humor in Negotiations & ADR: Cartoon Caption Contest Winners from the ABA Dispute Resolution Magazine

Humor in Trial Evidence: Cartoon Caption Contest Winners and Challenges from My Evidence Class

Military Rules of Evidence Handbook with Common Objections & Evidentiary Foundations

Negotiation and Mediation Communication Gambits for Breaking Impasses and More: What Do I Say When I Want To ...

The Pocket Guide to Common Trial Objections & Evidentiary Foundations

The following evidence books (for all 50 states and many other jurisdictions) in my Handbooks with Common Objections & Evidentiary Foundations series are available exclusively on Amazon for the following states:

Alabama	Idaho	Missouri	Pennsylvania **
Alaska	Illinois	Montana	Rhode Island
Arizona	Indiana	Nebraska	South Carolina
Arkansas	Iowa	Nevada	South Dakota
California **	Kansas	New Hampshire	Tennessee
Colorado	Kentucky	New Jersey	Texas **
Connecticut	Louisiana	New Mexico	Utah
Delaware	Maine **	New York	Vermont
District of Columbia	Maryland	North Carolina	Virginia
Florida **	Massachusetts	North Dakota	Washington
Georgia	Michigan **	Ohio	West Virginia
Hawaii **	Minnesota	Oklahoma	Wisconsin
	Mississippi	Oregon	Wyoming

Pacific Island countries and other U.S. affiliated jurisdictions	
American Samoa	Northern Mariana Islands
Chuuk	Pohnpei
Federated States of Micronesia	Puerto Rico
Guam	Republic of Palau
Kosrae	U.S. Virgin Islands
Marshall Islands	Yap

** I also published "Just the Rules" books for these seven states.

Massachusetts, Missouri, and New York do not have formal rules of evidence, but Massachusetts and New York do publish state "Guides" to evidence

The following international evidence books in the
Handbooks with Common Objections & Evidentiary Foundations series
are available exclusively on Amazon for the following countries, provinces, and
non-U.S. states:

The author has "self-published" all the above books.
They are available exclusively on Amazon.com and are "print-on-demand."

Australia	India **
New South Wales **	Korea **
Victoria **	Malaysia **
Bangladesh **	New Zealand **
Canada **	Nigeria **
Alberta **	Papua New Guinea **
British Columbia **	Philippines **
Ontario **	Singapore **
Hong Kong **	Samoa **
	UK (United Kingdom) **

** Also published "Just the Rules" or
"Just the Evidence Acts/Ordinances" for the above jurisdictions

To find John Barkai's evidence and cartoon books

1. Go to the Amazon website – www.Amazon.com

2. Enter into the search bar: - John Barkai

3. For a particular state, enter into the Amazon search bar
    - John Barkai [state name]

Dedication

To my wife Linda and my adult twin daughters Hope and Leah,
who bring me so much joy and enrich my life
and
to the hundreds of my former evidence and clinical students
who learned these rules of evidence with me
over the past 50 years
at the William S. Richardson School of Law
at the University of Hawaii
and
Wayne State Law School in Detroit.

About the Author

John Barkai was born and raised in Detroit. He has a B.B.A., M.B.A, and J.D., all from the University of Michigan. He is a former Detroit criminal trial lawyer with the Legal Aid and Defender Association of Detroit, a fulltime law professor for over 45 years - five years at Wayne State University Law School where he first received tenure, and a Professor of Law at the William S. Richardson School of Law at the University of Hawaii for more than 40 years. He has taught evidence since 1981 and has been the Director, and now Co-Director, of the Law School's Clinical Program since 1978. His students, under his supervision, at Wayne State and Hawaii have represented real clients in real cases every year he has been teaching. He is an active member of the Hawaii Bar, and has been a member of the Michigan and California bars. He has been a member of the Hawaii Supreme Court's Standing Committee on the Rules of Evidence since 1993 and has frequently taught evidence workshops outside the law school. This handbook was inspired by similar handbooks he created in 2019 for a workshop for Pacific Island Judges from American Samoa, Marshall Islands, Federated States of Micronesia, Chuuk, Kosrae, Pohnpei, and Yap, but this handbook has much expanded sections on objections and foundations. He has published over 100 evidence handbooks similar to this one for all 50 states as well as over 30 other jurisdictions from Bangladesh to the United Kingdom. He also has evidence and negotiation & ADR cartoon books on Amazon as well as a book on effective communication for negotiation and mediation.

Made in the USA
Middletown, DE
02 June 2024